Henry G Catlin

Yellow Pine Basin

The Story of a Prospector

Henry G Catlin

Yellow Pine Basin
The Story of a Prospector

ISBN/EAN: 9783744649148

Printed in Europe, USA, Canada, Australia, Japan

Cover: Foto ©ninafisch / pixelio.de

More available books at **www.hansebooks.com**

YELLOW PINE BASIN

THE STORY OF A PROSPECTOR

BY
HENRY G. CATLIN

NEW YORK
GEORGE H. RICHMOND & CO.
1897

COPYRIGHT, 1897, BY
GEORGE H. RICHMOND & CO.

Press of J. J. Little & Co.
Astor Place, New York

NOTE

Of this now fast closing century a picturesque and distinctively American character has been the prospector.

The discovery of gold in California awoke in their descendants something of that old ardor which two hundred and more years ago animated the early comers to North America.

From Maine to Florida sturdy, adventurous spirits felt the thrill of an inherited tendency which, for so long dormant, reasserted itself, and flocked to the new Golconda. The indolent, the timid, the conservative did not go; but when considerations of convenience, propriety, and duty allowed, the ambitious, assertive young men crossed the plains or took shipping for California.

On that distant Pacific coast assembled a community of young men, an aggregation of energy, physical strength, and enthusiasm never before equalled.

The wild spirits of youth, the absence of all restraint, the force of early education, the democratic temper mixed with the exhilaration of adventure and the intoxication of the gold thirst. Out of this medley of influences came a class marked and distinctive within the limits of an individualism pertaining to its component parts.

California was the rude school; the wider experiences of the great wilds completed the education.

The man who remained in California became provincial; it is not of him I speak.

The man who went out into the wilderness, his horse and pack mule, arms, provisions, and tools all he could call his own; led by an impulse stronger than love of ease, comfort, or life; his one all-absorbing idea the finding of the precious metals, which when found but urged him to further quest; that man whom neither cold nor heat, thirst nor blood could stop; broadened by diversified experiences, tinted with the coloring of varied climates, forged into a type by blows from opposing forces; the mountain wanderer, the tireless seeker,—of him I tell. Much as I regret that no better artist limns him, for he is worthy a master's pencil, I make no apology for my rude sketching. My acquaintance has been long and intimate with him, and while, perhaps, something of kindred feeling assures me that I know him well, it is only because he is a passing, vanishing figure in our American life that I am prompted to do my little to preserve his memory.

With such change of time, place, and sequence of incident as has seemed fitting to me, the story is a true one.

There may be those who, putting this and that together, may now know more of a simple secret long kept by a simple man; if so, old comradeship will, I know, keep their lips closed.

YELLOW PINE BASIN

CHAPTER I

"That ain't no bed-rock, Bud."

"It is all there seems to be."

"Well, pan her out and let's see how she prospects; I don't think ye'll raise a color."

Moving down the creek, Bud selects a still spot in the water, in the lee of a big boulder, and with a hand on each side of the iron gold-pan, holds it under the water and gives it that oscillating motion, the first movement in the process for determining the richness of the gravel in bright grains of gold, which among gold miners is termed panning. He stops, and with the fingers of one hand rakes off the coarser particles of the gravel with which the pan is filled, and begins again.

Bending over him, one foot in the water of the little stream, the other on its bank, and resting an elbow on his elevated knee, old Zeb awaits the result.

"You hain't give her no chance, Bud; this Salmon River gold is mostly on the bed-rock, and ye didn't have no bed-rock."

"I can see black sand and iron rocks and rubies, anyway; I think there will be gold. I don't know much about it, but it looks to me favorable for a prospect."

The gyratory oscillations stopped, and a new shaking movement brought to the surface the lighter sands, and, holding it on a slant, Bud dipped the pan in the water, lifting it again so that each receding of the water, like the ocean wave on some quiet shore, carried off its burden of sand, each wave reducing the volume in the pan; and after every dip came a shake, bringing to the surface other grains of sand, and other receding waves carried them away until only the heavier particles remained. Slowly went the final process of panning down. Under the covering of black sand lay the hidden probabilities, for Bud was too good a panner to show color yet.

"I tell ye, ye hain't give her no show, Bud. If she prospects at all, we'll go to bed-rock if we have to bale the water out the hole; but she won't, 'taint reason."

The end was coming; only a trifle of black sand remained in the angle made by the bottom and side of the pan. With a dexterous movement the black covering rolled away, and several bright grains of gold lay at the end of the sand, making a yellow tip to its sombre shade.

"What did I say? I said it would prospect."

"That's what ye did, Bud. I didn't think she would. Coarse gold it is too, and rattles in the pan," as he took up a grain and let it fall on the iron bottom.

"We'll go to bed-rock and we'll get her richer nor twenty-dollar pieces. I see the same lay in Californy in '50; no, 'twas in '51, on Dutchman Creek. Say, Bud, that gold's better nor eighteen dollars an ounce. That ain't no channel wash, nor no channel gold; the channel is yon by them porphry boulders. It ain't no man's place to say signs is nothing. Ye mind that she-bear we saw on Sulphur Crik, with the two cubs, one black and one brown? I told ye then we'd have luck; no man never saw them signs that he didn't have luck. Why, there was my pardner Yank, God bless his old soul! 'Twas in '49, late, me and Yank had jined and was working a claim; grub give out. Yank took the sack and went to town; rode a mustang hellion I had, and packed a pinto we borry'd from a Portugee who owned the 'jining claim—sich English as that cuss talked! Well, as I tell ye, Yank he goes for the grub, and as he crossed the divide, he saw a she-bear and two cubs, one on 'em black and one brown. Yank was free and easy like, had a few drinks when he come to town, and run up agin a game and lost the sack; twenty-four ounces, I remember. Next morning he felt dang'd blue. There was I and there was he with no grub; but he says, 'I'll chance it,' and in he goes to Hawkins & Co., the store-keepers, and says he, 'I wants some grub for me and my pardner, and I hain't no dust; my name is Yank; I sailed from Saco, Maine, a-whaling, and when we put in at the Bay I thought I'd try the mines.' 'The devil ye did,' says Hawkins. 'Ye can have what ye want; no Maine man comes to me for grub but he gets it.' Yank was that honest he says, 'But my pardner Zeb, he's from Injiany.' 'Well,' says Hawkins, 'he's in good company if he does hail from that ornery State.' I never knew Yank to lie; Yank couldn't lie; but he had been up all night, must have punished a heap of whiskey, for I knew his gait; ennyway he said that old Hawkins said that. Yank never had no conceit of Injiany nor any other State that wan't on the sea;

said they was no 'count. Says he to me: 'Why there's Maine and here's Californy, and both on 'em on the sea;' and what could I say? I couldn't argy with Yank, nobody could; he was that sort.

"So soon as old Hawkins said what he did, that she-bear and them cubs jumped on him and he knew 'twas luck. When he come into the gulch with the grub, Yank told me the whole thing. He was telling the Portugee when he come in our cabin that night, and the Portugee says: 'No good, losa dora, no good.' He meant, ye know, he had lost the dust. Yank didn't say nothing then, but he says to me afterward: 'How ignorant them Portugees are! It's a natcral thing for a man to lose at a game, but any dang'd fool knows it was luck to get that grub.' I see that p'int myself, for I had tried them games."

"There must be better ground than that higher up the creek, Zeb," broke in Bud.

"Of course there is; that ground above the swag is my fancy, over yon beyond the p'int. Then I was going out to Hangtown once, and I see a she-bear and two cubs, one black and one brown; traded off an old ring-boned mare I had for the finest hoss ye ever see; not a blemish on him; run like a deer. I took real comfort with that hoss 'till a man come along in about three weeks and proved it was his hoss, stolen from him; I give the man five ounces rather than part with him."

"The fall looks pretty good here, and there is plenty of water, and if it's only good on bed-rock, Zeb."

"Good, man; I tell ye 'twill be good; them signs never fail. I mind another time Yank sees a she-bear and two cubs, one on 'em black and one on 'em brown, as he was going to the Bay. Sold his interest out to me and took three hundred ounces with him to have a go at the Bay. Ye wouldn't believe it, but Yank hadn't been there two weeks 'fore he married a woman a butcher was courting, finest woman ye ever see, he told me. Butcher he was mad, and drew his gun on Yank unawares, and pulled the trigger, but the cap didn't snap. In them days, Bud, caps was all the go; no copper cartridges then. This gave Yank time to draw, and he plumped him dead as a door-nail. Yank said when he got the woman and when he got the man he seed that bear and them cubs. He told me many a time that winter, for he come up and stopped with me. He give the woman his sack, and when she got it all, she give him the go-by and left him without a color. 'Yer a woman,' says Yank, 'and ye have me; if 'twere a man 'twould be different;' and he wishes her luck and steps out. Yank was a gentleman, sand from his toes up; but no softer man to a woman ever lived, and that's why I say Yank was a gentleman in them times. He and I talked it all over. 'She was a lady,' said Yank, 'and I wasn't good enough for her; she's welcome to it all; how could I think she cared for a dang'd fool like me?' I see he was sour and I said nothing, but I thought she'd never find a better man, nor could she; for Yank was a gentleman, never lied, never stole. Yank was a Christian; that man knew the Bible from end to end. You couldn't stump him on no text; he fought for the weak, played a fair game, and was always behind his gun. Yes, a good man was Yank. He's in heaven now, and there ain't no better there; Yank was a man.''

"I don't care for black bears or cubs, or brown ones either; we will go down to bed-rock, Zeb, and if it's good there we will have a big mine, won't we?"

"Yes, that's the way I was, Bud; just like ye. Ye go the same gait, on the same trail. I didn't know nothing, didn't believe nothing, when I was twenty-five; sence then I've seed a heap in Californy, in Nevady, in the war, on the Fraser, in Montany, in Arizony, and down among the Greasers, and I have *sensed*. 'Pears like a man don't know nothing 'till he's sixty, Bud; I tell ye," and the old man's arm and hand and finger emphasized the moral, "signs is signs, and it ain't no man's place to say they ain't."

"Well, well, Zeb, let's go to camp, and to-morrow we'll tackle the ground."

The sun was setting in all the clear glory of an atmosphere which obtains nowhere else, save in the great inter-mountain country between the Rockies and the Sierras.

As they walked up the creek the graceful pine squirrels were yet hard at work in preparation for the long winter soon to come; running up the black pines, out to the end of the branches, testing the little cones, and as one seemed good to them, biting it off and watching its fall to earth; stopping only in their active labors when some robber of their own kind sought to reap the fruits of their honest toil, and carry to his own store-house the little pine burs. Then the squirrel in the tree would rush down, and with honest indignation and angry chattering drive away his predatory fellow. A lone butterfly before them flitted towards the willows where its bed and board were; belated hornets and a stray reveller of a black horse-fly, who should have been in bed an hour before, for they are early-to-bed folk, were on their homeward way. A startled grouse flew from their feet, and a bevy of fool hens gave them the road.

"Yes, we'll find it good on bed-rock, I'll bet; same lay of ground as Shirt-Tail Gulch, if she's only half as good. In '50 Yank and me took out three ounces to the man, but 'twas Californy."

"It's always California with you, Zeb; Idaho's good enough for me, and Yellow Pine Basin's as likely to be rich as Shirt-Tail Gulch."

"Yes, for Idaho; but there warn't but one Californy, Bud."

On the bench above the gently rising bank, with tall pines in the background, as they were thrown from the animals when unsaddled, lay in disorder two riding-saddles, two pack-saddles, rolls of blankets, shovels and picks, flour and bacon, two Winchesters and cartridge belts, and sacks of the goods that make up a prospecting outfit.

Throwing down the pan and the shovel as old Zeb dropped the pick used in their afternoon's work, the young man said: "You get supper, Zeb, and I'll look up the horses. I don't hear the bell," and started up the creek on his search.

His old companion put a log on the ground, and with the shovel scraped out a hole under it, gathered some pine branches with their dried needles from the trunks of the surrounding trees, threw on them some larger dry sticks, and soon had the fire started, and on it an old tin coffee can filled with water from the creek. The soap and a much-used and dingy towel were fished out of the "alfallcases" (the big box-like, rawhide pockets that hang on either side from the crosses of the pack-saddles), a convenience for the stowing away of all smaller articles, and at night, at one's head, a wind-break. Going to the creek, old Zeb washed his face and hands, and from the pocket of his woollen shirt took a bit of bone with a few straggling, uneven teeth, in their solitude but a remainder of what had been a comb, drew it through his gray hair, and muttered to himself: "Dang'd if we hain't struck it. I may see the States again, and Jane—Oh, you cussed old fool!—and Jane—My God!—and Jane. I'll go unbeknown and hang around till I see her. It's been a hard pull, but, thank God, she nor hers hain't wanted bread, any way."

On the old man's rugged features played the last rays of the setting sun; weather-beaten with the storms and wear of forty years of border life, seamed and scarred by steel and lead was the canvas on which a something—mind, heart, soul, spirit—the inner self, with master brush painted out the ravages of time, the scars of conflicts, the marks and blemishes of hardships, leaving on the worn face something of peace and quiet and beauty that would have made one wonder at the transformation.

Down behind the mountains sank the great kindly sun; back into their old shapes went wrinkles and scars; into the locked cabinet of the old man's heart went the vanished picture, "God bless her."

"You are the dangd'st old fool, Zeb!" and with that Zeb went back to his fire.

It may be that there exists in the heart of every one a desire for companionship, or it may be merely that the sound of a human voice, if it is only one's own, is a need of human life. Whatever may be the cause, men who are much alone are given to talking to themselves. Not only in civilized, but also in savage man is this a habit, generic in the species; solitude develops and brings out this innate tendency.

Busying himself cutting slices of bacon, making the bread, putting the coffee in the boiling water of the old can that rested on a bed of coals before the fire, its sides worn and blackened from the wear and soot of open-air cooking, the primitive meal was prepared, with many a varied oath and curse on the fire, that one minute sent its smoke one way, and another to a different quarter.

"'Twill storm soon, and I'll bet this is a snowy country. Dang it, if we ain't struck it, and mightly slick it comes, too. You'll be on your feet agin, Zeb; we'll make a ingineer of him; Jane had a head, and her boys are smart, I'll bet ye."

So with vivid blasphemy at the fire and his cooking, and with his kind old heart planning what good things in the future he saw before him, or thought he saw (for to men of his kind belief is as a mathematical demonstration), would bring to those he loved, the preparation of the meal proceeded.

"I'll know she has silks, and diamonds too, afore I die; and the little girl that has music in her, she shall have a melodeon, and a pianny too, by gum! And I'll lift the morgige on Jim Peasley's farm, for the letters he has wrote me, and how he's been good friend to me, and how slick he's managed it all, and she suspicioning nothing—Dang the blamed fire!" as a coal fell in the coffee and a gust of smoke filled his eyes—
"And me?" as the incident of the coal passed from

his mind, "and me? Well, there ain't nothing for me only to know she's peart and comfortable."

"Why, Uncle Zeb, supper all ready! The horses are all right, in good grass, about a mile up the creek;" and with this announcement Bud drew up to the fire.

"Is old Bally quiet, or is he a-running around, throwing up his head and acting oneasy?"

"Oh, no; he is feeding quietly with all the rest."

"I'm glad of that, Bud, for the fire says storm; but I'll put old Bally agin any fire for sensing the weather."

The bread was turned from the frying-pan in which it had been baked to a canvas pack-cover; the other frying-pan, with the bacon still sizzling, was drawn up; the coffee was poured out, and the two sat down to the evening meal.

"I'll say this for you, Zeb, I never saw such good bread as you make," as, sopping pieces of it in the frying-pan, Bud made the bacon grease take the place of butter.

"Oh, that ain't nothing; I kin do right smart with sour dough, but this yer baking powder, I hain't no great conceit of it. 'Bout the making of it, all there is, is the stirring; ye mustn't stir too much or too little. I'll tell ye something, Bud, I hain't told no man. I used to make the doggondest bread ye ever see when this yer baking powder first come; couldn't seem to git no savey of it. One night I was camped in the Big Horn country and was a-goin' to make bread. I put in the flour and the salt and a handful of baking powder, and the water, and—'twas the singularest thing—there come into my mind old Mis Yerrence;

hadn't thought of her for years. Me and her boy Bill Yerrence was thick when we was young, and I uster go to her house, and I'd see her stirring up something, and she was always a-singing, and always the same thing. She didn't know but two lines, and she'd sing 'em over and over, and when I put my knife in to stir up that baking of bread, I began singing to my self her old song:

> "'I would not live alway,
> I care not to stay;'

and then again:

> "'I would not live alway
> I care not to stay.'

Just twice I sang them lines, and sort of flopped my knife when I come to 'stay' and 'alway,' and with that I stopped stirring. I was surprised; that was as fine bread as I ever eat; wouldn't choose no better. I tried it agin, 'twas the same, and sence then when I stir the baking-powder bread I say them words; twice I say 'em, Bud; ye want to make long stir at 'alway' and agin at 'stay' and yer all right. I suppose there must be lots more of the song, but I never heerd only them two lines. 'Tain't no matter, them two's all that's any good; curous, ain't it? You try it and you'll find them words naterally strike the gait to stir bread on. I like ye, Bud; yer a boy and ye hain't got much sense, but 'twill come; and I kin tell ye had good bringing up, and a good mother; I kin tell it."

As the color came in the young man's face, old Zeb put his hand on his arm, saying: "Now, don't tell me nothing; I ain't asking nothing; I don't want to know nothing. I bet ye never stole, nor didn't act squar with a woman. Ye never drew gun when ye hadn't cause, an' if ye did pull trigger in fair fight, tain't in me to think the worse of ye, boy. We're pardners, and the more I think of it, Bud, I know we'll get it rich on bed-rock. I tell ye that she-bear and them cubs didn't come our way for nothing, and I see the colors in the pan was chunky. Why, if 'twas only a foot 'bove bed-rock it's as good a prospect as I ever see out of Californy and Confederate Gulch and Williams Crick."

The dishes belonging to their homely out-door kitchen were soused with hot water and turned on edge to dry. By the light from dry branches thrown on the fire, the blankets were spread on as level a spot as the vicinity afforded; the "alfallcases" were placed at the head of the bed, and all house-keeping affairs for the day were over.

Responsive to the throwing on of other dry branches, the fire gave out its cheery light, its grateful heat, and, more than that, the peculiar fascination of the camp fire itself. There is heat, there is light, in a camp fire, but that is not all; there is something else. An emanation comes from a camp fire as potent, as much a tangible entity, as a current of electricity, the one as unseen as the other, both of them alike, both a something equally unexplainable; they are because they are.

When after the meal is over, and the pipes are lighted, and the fire burns up brightly, what mystic spell some goddess of the fire conjures up to throw upon those around, her subjects all!

The brawler and the desperado under its gentle influence are quiet; the peevish man, if such there be, forgets his little ills; the trials and the dangers of the time, the fears for the future, all are softened. It has assuaged defeat, it has mollified exultant victors. The thirst of a dry camp in Arizona, an Idaho snow-storm, the cold of Montana and Dakota yield to the charm of the fire.

There comes over all within the circle of its rays a softening; the doors of the past fly open, even those of the burglar-proof vaults that lock into their secure recesses the precious, the dangerous, the humiliating secrets of human hearts; turn on hinges often rusty and creaking from disuse. The man is a child again; his mother's hand rests on his head; his father's voice rings in his ears; his boyhood's joys, his young manhood's hopes and aspirations, the failures, the loves, the hates—all the life he has passed, goes through his mind.

The witchery of the camp fire, by some law of magic, has power only over the past. The future, with all its entrancing prospects, its unexplored lands of promise girt round with the mountains of doubt and uncertainty, it leaves to darkness or to sunlight. By firelight, under open skies only, has it full sway and rule.

There is something of this before a fireplace within walls, but it is not there that we come so completely under the dominion of the fire queen. The very throne itself has great pines, or modest mesquite, or lowly sage brush for its walls, and all of heaven for its ceiling, either in the balmy air of summer evening or in storm and wintry blast; not hemmed in by the works of man, but in open air holds the witch queen her court.

No voice breaks the silence about the fire; with monotonous regularity the smoke from the pipes puff out. Our two wanderers in this perfect human silence paid homage to the influence, as did, when the race was young, Assyrian tent-dweller and Chaldean shepherd.

"It's time to turn in, Zeb," at last said Bud. Again he said: "Bed-time, Zeb."

"Yes, Bud," as the old man knocked the ashes from his pipe, "I was a-thinking, Bud; I was a-thinking."

The fire was drawn together; the long, deep draught of water, the mountain man's nightcap, drunk; the boots drawn off and put down at the head of the bed as a foundation for a pillow, the superstructure of which was such odds and ends of raiment as coats and overalls, and down lay the partners.

"What's come to me? We didn't pile the saddles."

"It won't storm, Zeb," reassuringly says Bud.

"No, it won't rain, but 'tain't no way to camp. By gum, I've forgot my gun! I hain't been so off in forty years. I was thinking, Bud," and up got old Zeb, and in frontier fashion took his gun, looked it over, saw that a cartridge was in the chamber and the barrel clear, and lay down with it at his side.

"Do you think we had better put down a hole where we got the prospect, or sink one higher up?"

"I'll give the ground a keerful look in the morning and we'll see. Yank uster say I had the best sense in getting a place to sink a hole of any man he ever see. It may be pretty deep to bed-rock."

"I don't care if it's a mile," said Bud, "we will get there."

"You bet, my boy, we'll get there, and we'll get it

rich. I tell ye signs is for it." And with that old Zeb dropped into silence, and from silence into sleep.

Thinking over the events of the day, and speculating on what the future might bring forth, the young man's thoughts kept him longer awake; but soon the healthy animal in him conquered, and he added his deep breathing to old Zeb's sonorous snore.

As the bird flies, in any direction it was sixty miles to any being of their kind; over a hundred to any dwelling, even to any cabin; yet in peace and quiet slept these men—quiet unbroken, save by the screeching of an owl, the distant cries of wolf or cougar, and at times the faint tinkling of a bell up the gulch, as the mare who bore it moved her head in feeding.

CHAPTER II

In the heart of a country perhaps to this day as inaccessible as any in our great West are the head waters of the Salmon, the Payette, and the Boise, with their many forks. The beginning of these streams, following the low lines in the tortuous mountain ranges which radiate from what seems almost a common centre, run in all directions; they pass each other, they run around each other. A spring near a mountain peak sends forth its trickling stream, other lower springs add to it, it becomes a rippling thread of water, it grows into a tumbling creek; distance increases its volume; it has gotten to be a fork. On it rushes till it is a river, then a larger one; and other rivers, born of other mountain springs, join it. On it goes, ever increasing, until, whether it be Salmon or Payette or Boise, it makes union with the Snake, and then with stately flow pours itself into the mighty Columbia, and the drop that left the little spring on some Idaho mountain may moisten the sands of far Cathay.

On one of the forks of the Salmon, up a creek, lies Yellow Pine Basin. As altitude goes, it is low enough for the great yellow pine to lift its lofty head and thrive, while high enough for the black pines on the more elevated ground about it. Wherever your eyes turn, a great wall of mountains ridge the basin;

creeks flow among the low hills and through the grassy flats, but on all sides is the great rim of lofty hills. The river cañons through it, but its winding course shuts one off from seeing far, and all seems impenetrable mountain side.

At the time of which I am writing, the Indian troubles of 1876 to 1879 were over, and Bannocks, Shoshones, Sheep-eaters, etc., were closely confined to their various reservations. Idaho had for nearly twenty years been a "gold country," and prospectors had run through it. Attracted by its reputation, the older of the two sleeping men had started early in the spring from the Arizona country for a prospecting trip to the north, to include a portion of western Montana and central Idaho.

Camping one night near the great Tetons in Montana, a young fellow came up and made camp alongside. Quite naturally, he strolled over to old Zeb's camp; a mutual liking sprung up, and, as the young fellow evidently had no particular line of wandering planned out, their issues were joined, and both started next morning to explore a country which, from the tale of some old comrade, who had been in it in '63 and '64, old Zeb had set his mind on looking into. The two or three months previous had been spent in crossing into Idaho, prospecting along the main Salmon, giving Stanley Basin and the creeks on both sides an examination. They sunk numberless holes to bedrock, others until the water drove them out, finding gold here and there, but nowhere enough to pay for the working in the rude way they must perforce work.

Further acquaintance had begotten increased respect

for each other. The simple, good-natured old mountaineer had found in the youth and comparative inexperience of the young man a pleasing companion; a ready imbiber of such practical knowledge of prospecting and general campaigning as a long life of wandering had made him master of. He had taught him to pack till he could throw the diamond hitch as well as any one, and the squaw hitch he was perfect in, both of these accepted means of fastening the packs tightly upon the pack animals. The thousand and one little matters of horse care and camping, of making way through a country without trail, of camp cooking, of the proper place to dig a hole for getting a prospect, of the panning out of the prospect, of the carriage and use of the Winchester, the location of a camp and feeding ground for the horses, how to picket horses by the neck or leg—in all of these Bud was a quick learner; and the aptness of the pupil was most gratifying to the teacher, while the mystery of how one so unused to and inexperienced in the simplest matters of such a life could have been picked up by him in the wilderness, seemed to increase an interest other than that produced by the young fellow's hearty, manly ways. But however much he wondered at it, and even how much curiosity he may have felt as to his past, no thought of inquiry into it ever came to Zeb; if it had, he would have dismissed it as a most unworthy idea.

Whatever he was or might have been, "Bud," for so on the first evening of their acquaintance he had said "they might call me," had taken a measure of the old pioneer, for old Zeb was as clean cut as a shell cameo, and like one built up of many layers, and must have seemed to one unused to men of his kind a revelation.

Learning, culture, art, fashion, the force of public opinon take a boy and leave him a man. They may make him a man of knowledge, of affairs; they round the rough points; they soften the harsh outlines; and within the limits of talent, of genius, of sound sense, of patriotic feeling, of generosity, of honesty; and of ignorance, of stupidity, of folly, of baseness, of avarice, of cupidity, a man is produced; one to outward seeming very like another, and the philanthropist and the villain are as like as peas in a pod to the casual observer. The absence of learning and culture, art, fashion, and sway of that public opinion which is largely but the creation of these, leaves nature to work out its laws, and the boy grows into the man, and the man lives as does a forest tree. You see an evergreen growing on its native hillside; you see the same evergreen in a hedge cut and trimmed and fashioned. We have different tastes: to some the wild tree seems the more interesting object of the two; to others, doubtless, the hedge with its uniform cut is more pleasing. But perhaps Bud had seen many hedges and few wild evergreens. At any rate there was something in the old man that attracted and interested him.

The two had come upon Yellow Pine Basin in their wanderings, camped, and with pan and pick and shovel had gone along a little creek and sunk the hole where we first found them.

As early morning broke, they arose, and, fortified by more bread and bacon and coffee, went down the creek, when, after proper weighing of the surface indications, the old man selected the spot, and they both set to work to dig a hole, with the intention of sinking through the ground and finding solid bed-rock where grains of gold should be heaviest and most numerous.

With pick and shovel, "spelling" each other at the work, their sinewy arms, in motion until dark, threw out big rocks and little ones, sand and earth; every hour or two filling the gold-pan with the gravel, which one or the other would pan; the result of each such operation, by increasing the richness of the prospect, confirming the value of the find.

There was little talk, for the veriest tyro knows there is no luck in talking over much in a prospect hole. When dark came they had not reached bed-rock, and the water in the hole began to be troublesome.

The next day, as they were getting too deep for a man to easily throw out the dirt, they widened the mouth of the hole for a few feet down, and thus formed a kind of shelf, up to which one man could shovel, and then the other might throw to the top of the ground; besides, in bailing out the water with the gold-pan, this shelf allowed a full pan to be lifted from one to the other and then emptied. This took time, and the water was increasing, so that only two feet in depth was made that day. As the two went to camp, Zeb broke out:

"I suspicion we ain't going to get bed-rock this way; two foot or so will let us out."

"We can't give it up so, Zeb; we must find bed-rock with such a prospect."

"Did ye say give her up, Bud?" said the old man in surprise and with no little indignation. "I never yet started on such a prospect but I made the bed-rock;

I'll go to Chiny, but I'll get it. I kinder suspicion, though, we've got to tackle her in shape and run a cut to drain the hole. It's a long pull, though, to get the grade. I wish to the Lord 'twas June 'stead of September, and nigh the last, too. This is a cussed country for snow, I know. I see the snow mark on the cottonwoods and she falls deep, and I am a-feered she falls early."

"Yes, this is the 28th, Zeb, or thereabouts. Let's see; we were at Stanley on the 19th, for I asked the day. Sunday, the 19th; we camped at the Rawhide that night, Cape Horn the next night, into Bear Valley next day, that would be the 21st; Sulphur Creek next day, that was the 22d; we were there three nights, making it the 24th, and, you remember, I said when we came here, this makes three days from Sulphur Creek, so that was the 27th. Why, Zeb, this is the 30th, but it's only September."

"Yes, I know, Bud, it's only September, but ye don't know these mountains. Why, I've seen three foot of snow in September, and lost every hoof I had before November, the snow come so fast and so deep. But I don't fear no such thing now, the ground squirrels holed too late. But there's work into winter, and ye've got to settle it right now. Stay or get out, Bud. If ye wants to go, Bud, ye had better go soon, 'taint no country to trust too much after this. I'm going to camp here for the winter, if so be we don't get bed-rock before."

"Now, Zeb, don't talk that way. I want to stay with you. I am going to stay right here with you. Since I met you in Montana and we agreed to go together, three months ago nearly, we've gone over a great deal of country and have found nothing good before. I want to see what this is; besides, I have come to like you, Zeb, and if you are willing, I want to stay with you and put this thing through."

"Yer a good boy, Bud. I wants no better pardner, I'll say that; but yer young, and young men has idees of wintering where folks cares for them and where they care for folks."

"I tell you, Zeb, no one cares where I winter or summer either, and I don't—well, it's all the same to me."

"Bud, there's my hand on it. We'll get bed-rock in two days if we can, but we'll get it if it takes all winter. We can run the cut if we do have to shovel snow every morning, though snow don't drift here as it does in a rolling country."

Their hands were joined, thus signing and sealing the agreement. Parchment is covered with legal phrase, signatures of contracting parties are affixed and red seals put on to emphasize the act; witnesses attest the signing, officers of the law take acknowledgment of it, and in huge volumes of the record is a copy made; but two honest hands joined in simple fashion, after simple word, make a bond of steel when often the other is but straw.

That night these two talked it all over.

"There ain't no use talking 'bout getting in grub. I've got a silver dollar and a four-bit piece, and I know yer light in the sack, Bud. We ain't in no shape to get out a grub stake, and 'twould take two weeks or three to go out and pack in grub if we had all the money in the world. We can't spare the time. What a dang'd lucky thing it was that I loaded old

Bally at Sawtooth. There's nothing like having plenty of grub. When a man's got his gun and his animals and his grub and his tools, he's fixed in any country."

An inventory of their joint stock was taken. There were three fifty-pound sacks of flour and part of another. They "hefted" the bacon and judged there was about thirty pounds of it; three tins of baking powder, ten unbroken packages of coffee and more; and, as Zeb said, "the bones of the whole business," two ten-pound sacks of salt. So much for the commissariat. Besides this, they had three picks, two shovels, two gold-pans, an axe, and another smaller one; two Winchesters, with cartridges and three hundred rounds of forty-five-seventy ammunition; part of a bottle of Mustang liniment, thirteen and a half plugs of tobacco, seventeen cartridges of giant powder, a few five-eighth-inch drills, and a striking hammer; fifty feet of fuse, a box of giant-powder caps, two candles, pieces of soap, and a few packages of matches; three canvas pack-covers, three pack-saddles, two riding-saddles, with bridles and blankets, and swing and cinch and picket ropes. Of individual property, Zeb had an old Testament (much worn as to the binding, but spick and spank within, wrapped in a piece of buckskin); a buckskin sack with the contents unknown save to himself. Each had woollen outer and inner shirts and drawers, and China handkerchiefs, and socks, besides what they had on; sewing-bags, with needles and black linen thread and beeswax and such like trifles; boots, rubber and leather, and each a warm coat. Of course there were hunting-knives and a horse-shoeing outfit, and then there was the cooking outfit—two frying-pans, an old coffee can, an empty ten-pound lard can, two steel forks and one knife, another one having been carelessly left at some camping place, three tin plates, and an iron Dutch oven.

Of course Zeb had a dollar and a half and Bud a quarter of a dollar; but, as Zeb remarked, "That's more nor we can spend, and a man can't be no richer than that."

After talking it all over, these things were to be done, Zeb, from his experience, announcing them in order: The cut was to be run, and that so as to drain the water fifteen feet deeper than the present bottom of their hole, now dignified by the appellation of shaft. Other things were to be done accessory to the main thing, but none the less necessary, and they involved time in the doing. There was a cabin to be built, a supply of meat was to be put in before the elk and deer left the country for the winter, for until the far-away spring came, they must live mainly on meat, fresh, salted, and jerked. The horses, too, were also to be taken to some lower country where they could winter; they judged a fit place for them could be found forty miles or so down the Salmon, where they could turn out the animals and find them fat and strong in the spring, but they need not go there with them until the storms began, so that was off their minds, for a time at least.

"I will go with a couple of packs, Zeb. Yes, I'll go to-morrow night to the big lick we saw. It can't be ten miles from here, and I'll get the venison we want."

"That ain't no go, Bud; deer don't go to licks this time o' year; when the browse and weeds are green and full of juice, a deer hankers after something salt; when they get old and dry he don't want none. You might stand in that lick from now to Christmas and ye wouldn't see a deer. The bucks have come down from the high rocks where they have been a-laying in the sun a-drying their horns, and are a-running. Now, or a few days before storm, they will be in the low hills, kinder oneasy; one eye out for browse, the other on the weather, and both on 'em on the does. Come a little snow, and out they put, bucks, does, and fawns. 'Twon't be no trick to get plenty up the crick or on the low hills; elk sign is all round, too. I heered a bull call nearby."

It was decided to first lay out the "cut," this meaning a trench, the bottom of which should leave the surface of the ground far enough below the hole they were digging to drain the water from it fifteen feet below its then depth, for, on examination, they found this was as deep as they could drain the hole or shaft, on the grade necessary, without making too long a cut; and, even as it was to be, it made a long cut, and much labor would be required to complete it.

The first thing was to make sure of the meat, so the next morning, after having, in a rough way, surveyed the line of the cut and located where to begin, Bud went to work on it, and Zeb, with his Winchester and long hunting-knife, went after deer. It had been a frosty night. The laying out of the course of the cut had taken time, so the sun was high when the hunt began.

CHAPTER III

The hunting of game resolves itself under three heads: hunting for pleasure, hunting for profit, and hunting for both pleasure and profit combined.

I question if a true sportsman ever went forth to kill so inoffensive and harmless an animal as a deer, a creature whose very size makes strong protest against its wanton destruction, without some such feeling as this: "The venison I hope to get will be of use to my friends or to myself; it will not be wasted;" and saying to himself: "I will kill a deer because I have use for it."

The man who goes out to kill deer for the mere pleasure of seeing them drop, leaving their carcasses to rot where they fall, lacks in every fibre of his being the sportsman's soul. He is not of that ancient and honorable guild; he is a butcher, plain and simple, despised by all true followers of gentle and manly woodcraft.

The hunter for profit, truly his way of life is not what we or he would wish; but nevertheless he may have the instincts, as he has in some degree the pleasures, of a sportsman.

Many years ago I camped one night near a party, an Englishman—a nobleman—his guides, and among them one—we will call him Jim Stevens—a hunter, who killed deer and elk, and sold the meat; a pothunter, as men call them. In the morning we all rode on a bit together. The Englishman told me with great glee that he had killed nine elk the previous day, leaving them, all but one, where they died. As we rode on, Jim Stevens came alongside, and, when we were somewhat by ourselves, the rough, rude plainsman said to me: "It's awful to kill an elk and leave him to rot. I'm sick of it. I am going to quit this outfit." And I thought, as my eyes rested on this lordly butcher, You may be a peer of England, but you are not the peer of Jim Stevens.

But the hunter who goes forth to hunt, justified in his own mind because there is a use to be made of the game he may kill, into what paths of noble pleasure does he not stray? Here does eye and brain, hand and heart work together. It is being a man; all his faculties come into play—his reason, his craft, his patience, his steadiness of nerve, while, at the same time, in some degree, all the physical powers are exercised. This man feels his God-given dominion over the beasts of the field.

With springy step and brightened eye, for he is going a-hunting, Zeb went up the creek. Low foothills came down to the little valley and rose back to lofty mountains, and with the knowledge born of experience the hunter turned up into the hills. Soon a doe scampered past him, startled by his movements; but no good man would kill a doe if there was a fair chance to get a buck, and so she bounded away unscathed. At last he took his ground on a hillside with willows at the bottom, and scattered pines here and there over it, through which the autumn sun found spots of bare earth to brighten. Near a large tree he sat down as motionless as its trunk, his rifle where he could quietly and quickly raise it for a sight. He might have been there ten minutes when a rustling of the underbrush was heard, and within forty yards of him came out a four-point buck, fat and sleek. Unconscious of his surroundings, he stopped in a sunny spot and began the antics of the buck dance. He jumped up, and gathering his feet well under him, struck the ground with all four at once; he lowered his head and made feints and passes with his horns at a neighboring tree, perhaps practising for combat with some rival who, to his jealous mind, seemed too ardent in his attentions to mutual acquaintances among the does; or perhaps he was getting the most of the play in the warm sunlight that his instinct told him would go into clouds, and they into storm, when it would be cold, cheerless work to get a living until spring and sun came again.

Zeb watched him with interest, as who has not done when he has caught a buck when he thinks himself so much alone that he can make a fool of himself to his heart's content. What pranks and capers does his seeming privacy give occasion to!

The man he saw, but he was as the trees, motionless, and he had no more fear of him than of them. At last Zeb thought of the meat that must be had, and with a sharp whistle he raised his Winchester, and as the buck threw up his head, put the bullet through his brain. In a minute he was on him with his knife; the knife went to the right place in his neck, and death came quickly. Over a dry log he threw the body and prepared it for packing to camp, separating the sides with a stick between them. Leaving the venison he went after other bucks. One he killed on the run; and a pretty shot it was, for the buck was in the timber thirty rods or so away and running behind intervening trees. Quickly measuring the distance with his eye, and gauging how high above the ground his heart would be when he came out from behind a certain big tree, he took aim and pulled trigger when he could first see his horns, and bullet and heart met when the buck's body appeared, though the target was hidden when he fired. A man who has made that shot knows how Zeb felt.

I suppose as things go in this world the Czar of Russia has power and wealth and would himself confess to being in a most comfortable situation, so far as place goes. The Presidency of these United States is a position of honor, of power, of some financial value; a grand recompense for praiseworthy ambition. The Rothschilds—the total of the Rothschilds I mean—are rich in silver and gold, and wield the power such baubles bring in this commercial age; but there are brief moments in a man's life when Czar and President, even the money kings, are of the common herd; they are not envied; they beget not even the most languid interest in themselves or their surroundings, one feels so much above them all. So Zeb felt as he went up to that buck, and so, I presume, felt some other man or men, ages ago, when Alexander, Cyrus, or Crœsus stood for power, position, wealth, and all that seemed fullest of the great and the good things in life.

To those who have never made the shot, or whose interest in the hunt is dead, or who never felt the promptings for the chase, I can say it was a good shot, a grand shot; one a man tries many times before he makes it at all, and is never so sure of making that his heart doesn't swell when he does make it.

Other bucks were killed, and so near the camp were they all, that before dark six fine deer were hanging on the trees back of it.

Bud had made fair headway at his work, and nearly enough meat was in hand. They would get more from time to time before the great storms came. A cabin was to be built, and the fine weather ought to be taken advantage of, so that evening it was decided that the young man should cut suitable trees next day for house logs, and Zeb, having been "a-playing all day," as he said, would turn in and make dirt fly on that "yer cut." When the logs were cut, and snaked by old Bally to their place, both would work together and build the cabin and fireplace, and put the roof on.

In a few days the logs were ready on the site selected, the venison was in process of jerking, and the cut had made a most satisfactory progress.

Hard toil brought good appetites and long sleep, so that after work, bread, venison, and coffee, and a smoke brought them to bed-time.

The weather was all that could be desired, so they felt reasonably sure of having a roof over them before the snow began.

A cabin sixteen feet by eighteen feet had been decided on, and when the logs were all on the ground, they set themselves to build it. The logs were notched, and set into each other at the corners, not to leave too wide a space between them to be filled with the chinking. With rock and mud a fireplace was built, with a good chimney of the same materials.

They split shakes for the roof, finding a tree to make them of so straight grained that the shakes split from it were almost as true as if they had been sawed, and made a roof as good as one of shingles. Having no nails, they were forced to pin them to the rafters with little wooden pegs, but that would do for a time well enough.

A canvas pack-cover made a door, or rather stopped up the door-hole, and another served in the same way for a window; for the floor, the ground was shorn of the sod and the dirt packed down; frequent sprinkling with water would make it smooth and hard. The cracks between the logs were chinked with pieces of wood rudely cut to fill them and then plastered over with mud.

Not a nail had been used, for they had none to use, and the only tool was an axe; but when it was done, it was comfortable. True, the door and the window, with the canvas coverings, were not impervious to the wind, but most of it was kept out. Such a house is not to be thought lightly of; it has its good points, and I doubt if the combined skill of the architectural designers could devise a more healthy, wholesome, house than a log cabin with a good roof and fireplace and a dirt floor; of course the floor must be high enough to have the dampness drain away from it. With this, and the house so constructed as to keep out the rain and snow, it can hold its own against any known form of habitation, so far as simple comfort and health go.

Then it was thought a meat-house to store the meat

and other stores in would be a good thing to have, and so in a day's time this was built a little distance away.

Another day and some evenings after that it took to build a bunk for each, and out of poles and deer hides with the hair on to make two chairs.

" 'Tain't like we'll have company," said Zeb.

In this building and fitting up Bud appeared to great advantage. He could handle an axe very deftly, and as that was all there was to work with, his handiness came into good play. Zeb was never tired of commenting on his skill.

"Did ye learn the carpentering trade?" he asked him, as he had just finished a chair. "I never see a better chair nor this."

"It ought to be a good chair, Zeb, for I've made it for you, and you ought to have a good chair; but I never had an axe in my hand until two weeks before I saw you."

"What's that ye say, Bud? Never had an axe in yer hand? Why, where were ye raised? Didn't ye have ter cut fire-wood? All boys has."

"I was born and raised in New York, and there's no fire-wood there to cut; at any rate, I never cut any of it."

"Well, that's a fine chair, and I thanks ye, Bud. I'll sit in it this winter and smoke and tell yarns. Some men can live without talking, but it ain't me. I'd like to hear 'bout New York, and you kin give me the lay of it. We'll be dang comfortable and sociable here, you bet. Was it New York town ye meant, Bud, or New York State?"

"Well, both, Zeb, for I was born and raised in New York City, and that's in New York State, of course."

One night everything was finished, and the cut had been worked on every day but three. Bud, who kept the run of the days, said something about everything being ready for Sunday.

"Is to-morrow Sunday?" said Zeb.

"Yes, it will be Sunday; this is Saturday night," Bud answered.

"Well, we'll keep Sunday; we won't work, we'll wash up and lay around and obsarve the day. A man should be pious once in a while; it does him good. Lord, if my old mother could see me most Sundays, a-working or a-travelling, how she would talk! We was all Baptists, and we was brought up that strict we hated Sunday. I'll never feel I'm right sure of salvation 'till I can get to hating Sundays agin. Now they're like other days, I can't get up no real hate at 'em. 'Tain't right, I know 'tain't right; somehow I always have something to do on Sunday, if I know when Sunday comes, and when a man is prospecting it's dang hard to be pious. Still, 'tain't no great thing, when you think of it, to knock off work on every Sunday and to keep from cussing one day out of seven, but it's onhandy, of course. Some men can do it. There was Yank; he never cussed on Sunday, never worked on Sunday, never did nothing; 'twas his day to wash up and go 'round camp. If there was a game, and luck was agin him or with him, didn't make no difference; ye'd think he was a preacher, he took it all so mild, and he was always a-shooting Bible texts out of him all day long. Often I heard him say on Sunday night: 'I've done my duty by the day,' and he'd feel so good and pious over it."

Sunday came, a beautiful day, and the clothes were

washed and the baths taken, and, in honor of the day, Zeb made a duff of deer suet and flour and sugar that was considered a triumph, and they went down the creek and fished, and looked at their work, and speculated as to how long it would take them to finish it. They aired their blankets, and cut dry grass for their bunks, and had the sewing-bags out and mended their clothes, and otherwise passed the day, as Zeb said, like "church folks."

The frequent pannings of the gravel as they drove in the cut were satisfactory, and they worked with good heart.

It might have been two weeks after their coming to Yellow Pine Basin when the weather, that up to that time had been mild and pleasant, began to show signs of a change. The horses, having appeased their hunger and recovered from the fatigues of the several days' travel before camp was made, had come up from time to time, as horses will under such circumstances, to lick whatever salt had been thrown out and to keep up that intimacy with their owners which to the equine mind of a prospector's animal seems the proper thing. Old Bally, a sturdy old horse, who for ten years or more had followed Zeb from Mexico to British Columbia, and for whose general knowledge and good horse sense his master had profound respect, was the leader of the little band. It was evident that something unusual was the matter with him. He ran about uneasily, throwing back his head, coming up to the cabin in the evening and during the night.

"We're going to have a storm, Bud. I kin tell by the way old Bally acts; but he don't think 'twill be very much or he would be a-pawing, and he don't paw none," said Zeb one evening, and in the morning there was a little snow on the ground, the first of the late season.

This seemed to remind them of various things to do, and one was to get more meat. Guided by the old man's advice, Bud went out, and the glee with which he brought in two deer while Zeb was getting supper after his work, showed that it was a new experience to him.

"I killed one of them with one shot and I shot the other three times," he said. "See that, Zeb; right in the heart; the other one I didn't get a good sight of, but I brought him after a while."

"Yes, that's a pretty shot in the heart, but let me tell ye, Bud, if ye can see the deer, the head's the place to aim at. If ye hit the deer, it's pretty sure ye kill him. If ye aim at the heart, it's a chance to hit it, for a deer's heart is small, but ye'll probably cripple him and he'll go off somewhere and die. If ye shoot at a deer and miss him, some other man may kill him in a year or in five, but if ye cripple a deer, don't do you nor nobody no good; it's waste, it's waste."

"That's so, Zeb, that's so. I never thought of that, but when I saw the deer, I fired at the heart, because in all the books I ever read it was always spoken of as the place to aim at; and I never killed but one deer before, and that was just before we met in Montana."

"Well, when a man's writing a book, it's well enough; anything goes then, but it ain't right, for the reason I tell ye. But them are fine deer, and you put in a good day. Ye'll get sense, Bud, 'twill come.

I never see a boy larn as you've done. I did a piece of work, too, beside that in the crick. I took the axe and went up the hill a piece, and cut a snowshoe tree; she's a beauty, too, straight grained is no name for it; and I split out enough for two pair."

"Snowshoe tree, Zeb? I don't understand."

"Snow's a-coming soon, and we've got to have some shoes, and it's little enough time for the wood to dry."

"Make snowshoes out of a log, do you, Zeb? I don't know anything about them."

"Ye don't; might have known that. Yes, we make 'em out of a log. Good fir's the best thing in this country to make 'em of. We'll tote the sticks down here and put 'em in the cabin where they'll dry, and in the evenings we'll make the shoes. I kinder thought, seeing ye are so dang handy with an axe, I'd ask ye to make 'em; it's slow work for me."

"You tell me what you want and how to do it, Zeb, and I'll try," said Bud.

In a day or two the snow went off, and though slightly colder, it was fine weather again.

The two worked hard at their cut, which had now begun to show the effects of two weeks' labor. They could still throw out the gravel, but as there would soon come a time when the dirt would have to be wheeled out, they had a wheelbarrow and wheeling planks on which to run the barrow to make. To make a wheelbarrow out of a standing tree with only an axe and a pocket-knife, draws no little on one's ingenuity, particularly when you haven't a bit of iron, not even a nail, to make it with, and takes time.

Wheeling planks are easier to make; you need only to cut the logs and hew them down with the axe. Fortunately, among Zeb's effects was an old grindstone, worn down until it was hardly a foot in diameter; this, lying under the pack-saddles, had been overlooked in the inventory taken, and strangely, too, for it was a much prized possession of the old man. A tree was cut down, and a rough wheel hewed out, which was to be finished some evening in the cabin, after it had lain there long enough to dry a little, and the other parts were roughly cut, to be fashioned and the whole to be made during the evenings. The wheeling planks, three of them, thirty feet long and about eight inches wide, and three or four inches thick, were hewed out so they might be drying and be less heavy to carry about. But one man was always kept at work in the cut. When both could work there, its progress was so much more satisfactory that they grudged any time spent away from it, but, of course, these necessary things had to be done. As soon as it was light the work begun, and only when it was too dark to see did they quit it.

Zeb was one of those wiry, muscular men whose vigor only extreme age seems to impair, and though he was "Old Zeb" from the coast to the Rockies, he was hardly sixty. Bud, though in the prime of young manhood, and a powerful fellow too, perhaps because hard labor might have been new to him, had all he could do to keep pace with the old man's tireless energy, and often went to bed fagged out, and arose stiff and sore next morning; but he was getting used to it, and made so good a hand that many were the compliments he received, and together they did the work of five men, for their hearts were in it and they wished to take advantage of the favoring weather. For a day or two there had been signs of storm both from Bally and the heavens, until one night they went to bed with the expectation of seeing the ground whitened again.

CHAPTER IV

The storm came during the night, but by morning the rifts in the clouds indicated clearing weather. Only a few inches of snow had fallen when Zeb put aside the canvas curtain and looked out.

"Let's go hunting, Bud; couldn't be no better time. I see bear sign all round here, and a couple of good skins would come mighty handy. They're prime now."

"That would suit me. I never killed a bear, and never saw a wild one, except those we saw that day. That's a grand idea, Zeb; I'd give anything to kill a bear," and the young man jumped from his bed.

After breakfast the guns were examined, the cartridge-belts replenished, and the knives whetted, Zeb taking great pains with his long, two-edged, dagger-like blade.

"When a man tackles a big bear, Bud," he said, "if he's got sense, he's got a long knife, a sharp-pointed one, too, and it must be where he kin lay his hand on it. Bears is hard to kill, and less the ground favors you, don't never shoot a grizzly less yer far enough away to put in a couple more shots 'fore he kin git at ye. Wound one of them fellers and he comes for ye like a fool hen flies; black or brown or baldhead ain't so bad. These yer Rocky Mountain grizzlies ain't like them in the Sierris, but they're nasty. That's when ye want yer knife and want it bad; when a bear's a-charging, less you can put a shot in his brain, you can't faze him; when he downs his head a little, and ye kin hit his eye and are spry enough to jump one side, ye have him. If ye miss the eye, the bullet's like to glance off his skull, and 'tis a shot takes nerve. After a man's forty, he hain't no business with that shot, and then few men has any business with a bear at that distance anyway. If ye make the eye shot and he drops as ye jump aside, there ain't nothing that sets a man up like that. Ye remember it all yer life; that's hunting. If ye miss, drop yer gun and draw yer knife, and if ye are quick and strike his heart ye may be lucky enough to get off with some bad scratches; it's yer only show.

"The sun will be out soon, and the bears won't move much; they like to sun 'emselves after a cold, wet night, and in this light snow we can track 'em easy. Still, bear is oncertain, ye can't reckon on 'em. We may strike a trail and have to follow it all day, so we'd better take some grub, case we have to be out over night."

When all was ready, a start was made, with Zeb in the lead, just as the sun began to come out from the clouds. The fog lay thick on the basin and the low hills, over which, towards the mountains to the south, their course lay. A sharp walk of an hour brought them to much higher ground. Below lay a great lake of fog, covering Yellow Pine Basin, and out from it, like islands, here and there, were the tops of hills, and down the mountain sides great detached masses of fog slowly settled.

Bud stopped and gazed on the picture below them,

which it took little stretch of the imagination to believe was a water scene.

"I feel as if I were looking down on New York Bay; it makes me think of home, or what was home. How strange it is," he said, "the things a man cares the least about thinking of come up to him so unexpectedly. If there is something he don't wish to think of, anything brings it to his mind. You can break yourself of every habit but that."

"That's so, Bud. Some things are like a sore thumb; ye forget all about it, and then yer thumb hits something and ye have to remember it. 'Pears to me I see a track up yon hill looks like it might be a bear track."

Going over to the hill, it proved to be a bear track, "not an hour old, too," Zeb pronounced it to be. They took up the trail, and in the excitement of his first bear hunt the gloomy look on Bud's face, the memory awakened by the lake of fog, gave place to one more suited to the emotion of the chase. They could see, as they looked from the small rise of ground they had mounted, the trail turning towards some bushes in the valley below.

"Now's the time I wish we had a couple of good dogs to go in and hold the bear till we could get a shot. He's down there among them bushes, and we've got to be mighty sly or we'll lose him. He won't move for a while and we've got to git on him. I can't see him, but it's a moral certinty he's behind the bushes. We're right with the wind; 'tain't like he'll see us. A bear mostly feeds with his head to the wind, and he's a-feeding on the browse, or he's standing in the sun. If he's feeding, we kin steal up on him; if he ain't feeding, only sunning himself, his eyes are half shut and his back is towards us where it gets the sun, but he'll hear quicker nor if he was a-chawing of the bushes. I can't see the trail beyond that big clump, and he's behind it, I bet ye. If we go down on him, chances are we won't git no good shot; we'll go over yon and come down as nigh him as we kin; the trees is thick there and we kin keep behind 'em, but don't make no noise, Bud. You foller me."

With this admonition and command, the old man, picking his steps, moved along the ridge until he came where the wooded point made down close to a little swag, and descended the hill among the trees, increasing with each step his caution, and as his inexperienced companion would strike some dry branch giving forth a cracking sound, muffled somewhat by its covering of snow, he would raise his hand in warning. Slowly, and making as little noise as possible, they had gone nearly down the hill, where, getting a better point of view, they could see, behind the bushes, a black bear, the sun shining on his glossy coat, which, in the snow, seemed, by contrast, black as ink. He was standing quietly, his side partly turned to them. They were screened by the trunk of a large pine, and not over fifty yards from the game was a similar friendly tree.

"We'll go to yon tree as sly as we kin, and ye take the shot, Bud. Aim at his heart and don't be narvous. Ye'll have a good shot. 'Tain't thirty rods. If ye miss, I'll be ready for him, but ye'll get him."

Stepping with the greatest caution, Zeb leading, they at last reached the tree. It seemed half an hour to Bud, whose nerves were all strung to a high pitch.

"Rest yer gun," whispers Zeb, "'gainst the trunk, take a good aim, and, as soon as ye kin, give him another. I'll be ready if ye miss. Keep cool and get a good bead on him; all the time ye want."

Evidently the bear was unconscious of his enemies. Bud took plenty of time, a projection of the bark on the trunk afforded him a fair rest for his gun. When he had the aim and his hand was steady, he fired.

The start given him by the unexpected noise and the blow of the bullet staggered the bear for an instant, and, before he could turn to run, Bud put in another shot.

"Ye've got him, Bud; see the blood; ye've hit the heart," said Zeb, as he lowered his Winchester, which he had kept in readiness to give the death shot should Bud have missed or failed to give a mortal wound. With the caution of experience, he restrained Bud, who would rush impetuously after the bear. "Go slow, Bud; go slow, there ain't no hurry," he said, and with his gun ready for the wounded animal, should he turn, he went down the hill. The blood on the snow showed the track. Something between a squeal and a grunt came from the next clump of bushes as they neared it. "That's the last of him," said Zeb, as parting the willows they saw the beast dying, and as they looked he was dead.

"What do you think of that, Zeb? How is that for my first shot at a bear? Right where I held for him; dead in the heart; and there's the other, a little too high," said Bud, as he found the holes which his bullets had made.

"Ye did well, Bud; ye did well. Ye'll make a hunter. I was a-watching ye. Ye was shaking when ye lifted yer gun, but when ye got the sight ye was steady as a rock. Ye'll make a man, Bud, ye will. When a man goes to shoot at game, or goes into a fight or anything that takes nerve, specially when it's all new to him, and he's kind of shaky, and when he puts in his shot, or when the fight comes, he's quiet and steady; he's a man. When he goes in cool and gets to shaking when the p'int comes, he ain't no use only to sit 'round a bar-room stove in winter, and hunt and fight with his tongue. I feel I know ye better now, Bud. I had an idee ye was a man before."

Praise like this from old Zeb, and his first bear, made Bud step on air. He stroked the thick long fur; he lifted a big paw with its pad and long claws, some of them worn from the tearing asunder of rotten logs in search of ants, always a toothsome delicacy to a bear's palate. He admired his size, his prime coat; it was his bear and it was his first one.

All of us who love the noble sport have killed our first bear, and no matter how sorry a specimen of its kind it may have been, a certain halo always clings around that bear. Subsequent bears may have been giants of the family, and may have tried our nerve and met their deaths by shots we will remember and feel proud of having made so long as we live; yet the first bear marks a red-letter day in the calendar of our lives. As Bud was a novice, the skinning of the bear fell to Zeb, who did it with a quickness and skill that showed his familiarity with the process; for there is one right way to skin a bear, and as many wrong ones as there have been, are, or ever will be novices to try it. The skin was left on a projecting limb of a black pine, and the hunt resumed.

"What do you think that bear would weigh, Zeb?"

"May be three hundred or thereabout; he warn't very big, but it's a fine skin."

"It seems so to me, Zeb; but it is a pity we can't use the meat."

"That's so, Bud, but 'less it's a cub, bear's meat's no good."

"Where will we go next, Zeb?"

"Well, I was a-thinking; 'twas snowing all night, and sence the sun come out a bear would naterally be a-feeding or a-sunning himself. It's 'bout time they was a-getting dry, and we'd better make for some water. There's quite a crick yonder, couple of miles or so away; we'll go over there and keep on the hillside up the crick, and it's like we'll get another."

Half an hour brought them to where they could overlook the tumbling waters of a creek as it rushed down its steep bed.

"Wind's changed so we kin foller along this side," said Zeb. "It's everything to be right with the wind; when it's warm or kind of moderate, bear has a keen scent. When it's freezing cold, seems they're like a dog, don't smell much."

"I never knew that, Zeb."

"Well, it's so; when it's cold, scent don't lie; but there's another thing that's so too. Most everything, bears 'specially, see farther and they hear better then; 'pears like it was sort of providential. What they lose one way, they make up the other. We'll keep the wind and we'll go still, and if we have any kind of luck we'll see one likely."

Taking this as a hint to stop conversation, Bud followed behind in silence. A half hour or more went by, the ascent and the increasing depth of the snow, as they got farther into the mountains, making progress slow and tiresome. They were forced, by the abrupt high bank of a little cañon, through which the waters of the stream were leaping and boiling, as in great jumps from rock to rock they ran in their channel, to direct their steps higher up the hillside. They had just reached a point where they might turn down and get nearer the stream, when Zeb's quick ear caught a rustling in the willows fringing the water below. With uplifted hand he enforced special caution.

"I hear him," he whispered; "he's gone in the bushes; he's come down along the bank and is looking for a quiet place to drink."

"May be it's a deer," suggested Bud.

"No, it ain't no deer; it's a bear, and a big one, too. Hear how he breaks down the dry willows as he moves; takes heft to do that. I'll go down and cross the crick below. If he comes out and is moving away, give him a shot, but don't ye stir otherwise till ye hear my shot; then work down and shoot if ye see him, but don't go too nigh, and keep ready with yer gun."

Zeb retraced his steps, and in a minute all sight and sound of him was lost. Alert to obey his instructions, Bud watched the bushes for the coming out of the bear. He could tell from the cracking of the dead willows and the swishing about of the green ones that he was still there, but he made no move to come out.

The time seemed long since Zeb had left him, and strain his ears as he would, he could hear no noise that might by any stretch of fancy have come from him. Once or twice he raised his rifle as the animal in his moving seemed likely to emerge from the clump of bushes; once he fancied that through the leafless screen he could see some gray mass. With his faculties strained to high tension, feeling that now he had a reputation to sustain, for the morning's affair had, perhaps, given him a certain conceit of what was to be expected of him, and anxious to stand still better with his friend, he experienced the sensation of troops only slightly inured to the experiences of war, who stand hour after hour in line, waiting to be sent into action, the distant sounds of conflict seeming to be calls for orders that do not come. It's wearing, waiting at such times, and it tries nerves new to such experiences, and minutes seem tens and scores. But, as in the customary accounts of such matters, "a gun opened to the left."

The sharp crack of Zeb's rifle was heard, and out of the willows came a gray monster. The first surprise had startled him into turning, but, like many a one before, man or beast, the impetus of flight was overcome by the idea of fight, and, rearing up on his giant haunches his massive body, with his fore legs clawing the air, the bear emitted growls deep and angry. Bud fired without touching him—not so strange a thing—for to a new hand to hit an object below is much a matter of chance, the tendency to lift the end of the barrel as he pulls the trigger is so natural. With the rashness of excitement, Bud rushed down the hill.

"Keep back, keep back," yelled Zeb, and he checked himself hardly ten rods from the infuriated animal, who, seeing his foe, made a mad rush for him. Bud pulled trigger again, but in his excitement he had forgotten to throw the lever and renew his cartridge, and only a dull click came as the hammer fell.

"Run down hill," yelled Zeb, and as the flying Bud tore past, the old fellow came into the open spot near the willows, and towards his other enemy charged the furious brute. Zeb dropped on one knee; he got up again, and rigid as marble he stood to meet the onset, man and gun as immovable as the rocks above them. With growls that pierced the air with their shrillness, and had the roll of thunder in them, swinging his powerful fore legs, every claw standing out ready to tear when the arm struck, came the great gray beast, wild with anger. He was almost at the end of the gun-barrel, and he lowered his head as he had his enemy within his fearful grasp. Sharp rung out the true old rifle, and before it fell to the ground, his knife out, Zeb jumped one side and drove it in the monster's body, whose clutching claws, as he passed, tore the shirt from the old man's shoulder and drew blood.

Borne by his impetuous rush, the bear was impelled onward; he stumbled, he fell, with a bullet through eye into brain, and the knife through his heart.

All happened so quickly that perhaps not a minute had elapsed between Zeb's quick call to Bud and the death of the bear.

Actuated by the peremptory command of the old man, he had torn down hill towards the creek, but as he was not one to leave a friend at such a time, when he realized what he was doing he stopped, and put a new cartridge in place, but too late to get in a shot before the bear was on his friend. The steady holding of his fire, the death shot, and Zeb's jump to the side and blow with a knife he saw, without being able to render any assistance. The torn shirt and lacerated shoulder with the blood trickling down it, gave him alarm, and Bud rushed up.

"Are you hurt, Zeb? Are you hurt?"

"'Pears like I am," said Zeb. "I feel so good, though, it don't count. I wouldn't ha' missed this for nothing. I bet I didn't touch the bone when I went through his eye, but for fear I had been onsteady, I thought I'd get his heart; ye can't take no chances with such a cuss as that."

"But you're hurt; see the blood."

"The shirt's worse hurt than I am. His claws kinder raked me, but that ain't nothing. Them cuts is no depth," and taking some snow, he wiped the blood away, and Bud bound the torn shirt-sleeve about the arm as well as he could. "I hain't felt so good, Bud, not for three years. That shot did me a power of good. I feel like I was young. I didn't know my hand and nerve was so steady. It ain't nothing for a young man, but when a man gets round sixty he has a conceit of such a shot, and it does him good all through. I feel like I've been a-hunting and made a good hunt, and a man can't feel more peart than to feel that."

They went up to the dead bear, a great silver-tip.

"I didn't know a bear could be so big," said Bud.

"Well, he is a big one; the biggest I ever see out of Californy; he'll weigh nine hundred or more."

And he was a monster; his great bulk, stretched on the snow, covered with long silky fur, brown near the skin, the end of each hair tipped with gray, loomed up like the carcase of an ox. As Zeb said, his bullet had gone through the flesh of his eye without touching the bone of the skull.

"What a fight he made! And, Zeb, why did you hold your shot so long? He was nearly on you; I thought you were going to be killed. What an old hero you are, anyway! You were like an iron man, so steady."

"Well, Bud, if I hadn't been steady then, I'd have been pretty stiff by this time. 'Twas the only chance to get that ball in his eye-socket, and to knife his heart if I missed. That was a dang spry jump, warn't it, Bud? I'll think of that long as I live. That's hunting; and I got off mighty lucky. But we must skin him now while he's warm."

It was no easy job, for their united strength could not turn the monster over, and it was only by using a long stick as a lever that they did turn him; but at last the skin was off and his great pads and mighty claws were preserved on it. Bud insisted on carrying the skin, no little weight it was, and as dark was fast coming on, they started back, picking up the other skin on their way. These skins, subsequently tanned with the hair on, made a great addition to the furniture of the cabin, ornamenting the chairs by day, and, if there was need for them, warm coverings for the beds.

Zeb's wounds proved little more than deep scratches, and soon healed; but the torn shirt, manage it as he might, he could not mend to his satisfaction, and, it having been a favorite shirt, he, in most picturesque manner, cursed the dead bear and all his tribe as, patiently endeavoring to unite the tattered shreds into some serviceable shape, he plied his needle.

CHAPTER V

ALTERNATE snow squalls and clear weather, increasing frost at night, and a growing chilliness when the sun was obscured by passing clouds, indicated the near coming of winter.

Continued labor began to give the cut they were running such good promise of reaching its contemplated end that our friends were encouraged to expect, within two or three months, should only ordinary storms impede, having it under the shaft. That it would be deep enough when it reached that point, or before, to strike the bed-rock they did not doubt. I say they, but it would be better to say Zeb did not doubt; for the younger man having no experience of his own to form an opinion, made Zeb's his. Should they strike bed-rock, they would hew out the sluice-boxes to carry off the gravel, and make the riffles to catch the gold, as, in the passage of the gravel through the boxes, the little grains, from their greater weight, would fall among them. They would bring in the water along the convenient hillside by means of a ditch, which, as it would be of no great length, they could quickly dig in the early spring. Should the cut not be low enough when it reached the shaft, they would drive it still farther if they could; but this view of the matter was not prominent in their minds, for they had quite settled on it that before, or when, the cut came under the shaft, it would be on bed-rock. All the hours of light were spent in hard work at the excavation.

In the evenings they worked on, and at last finished, the wheelbarrow. Quite an ingenious creation it was, considering the tools employed, only axe and knife, and that wooden pins had to answer in place of nails and screws, and that the journal boxes in which the shaft of the wheel ran were pieces of bone from the leg of an elk; true, the wheel was somewhat wobbly, and it did not hang as they wished, and it was cumbrous and heavy; but, on the whole, they were much pleased with it. Bud, especially; for his deftness with axe and knife was quite remarkable; and while Zeb might be said to be the designer, he was the builder. His ingenuity and aptness also showed itself in various little improvements in the cabin and its furniture—a washboard for their clothes; shelves, and many other things.

Zeb was no idler, and while Bud was engaged with axe and knife, he was pulling and kneading buckskin in the process of tanning, or cooking, or washing their woollen clothes, or making mittens out of buckskin already tanned. And so, by the light of the big fire in the fireplace, they kept hands and minds busy.

A long life, and much of it passed among stirring scenes, and all of it in a manner new and strange to his companion, was bit by bit unfolded, as Bud ingeniously drew the old man out, as from time to time he did, when supper was over and they had settled down to their evening occupations.

While it took little or no urging to get Zeb to talk —for, as he was wont to say, "I ain't one of them still fellers who don't say nothing, always a-thinking or looking like they was a-thinking; I've got to open my head"—he was singularly uncommunicative about his personal actions. He would talk by the hour of his old partner Yank, whose memory he tenderly cherished, and whose sayings and doings were his frequent theme.

He had "gone to Californy in '49," his wanderings had extended to every Western State and Territory. He had prospected in British Columbia and in Northern Mexico, had served in the war, and cuts and bullet scars on face and body marked him as one who had borne a part in making the history of his time. It needed but little imagination to connect him with what must have fallen to an adventurous pioneer in the great wilds, and less acquaintance with him to know that in whatever life he had moved he had acted his part like a man.

A rough idea of his life, it was true, had come to Bud from things the old man would drop.

"When I was in Californy in '49 or '50 or '51." "I had a claim on the Fraser." "'Twas in Nevady in '59." "I see a heap o' curous things down among the Greasers." "Montany is dang cold." "I never see nothing in Wyoming or Dacoty." "Colorado's all quartz." And a chance remark now and then about the war had come from him, and out of those disjointed remarks Bud had made a kind of chart of Zeb's life; but he longed to have the log-book of that life's voyage through the seas of peril and adventure it must have been sailed. But, like men of his kind, some chance allusion to this or that in which he had been an actor was all that passed his lips.

Perhaps no more uncommunicative class of men exist than the pioneers of the extreme West. One has to know them and know them well to draw from them statements of their personal experiences. In addition to a certain stoicism acquired either by contact with that greatest of modern stoics—the American Indian—or perhaps from somewhat like causes producing a similar result, they are of all men the most retiring, the least given to telling what they have personally endured or suffered or had part in. Their portraits, from those tintypes in the dime novels to the full cabinet size of more pretentious literary productions, are for the most part caricatures.

Can some penny-a-liner, in his lodgings, over toast and tea, or a pint of beer, with only his imagination to draw from, depict these men whom he has never even seen? Can some story-teller of the day, however graphic his pen, or fervid his fancy, or exhaustive his analysis of character, spend a few months, or a few years for that matter, in frontier towns or army posts, making excursions here and there into the wilderness, aiming to get in touch with these men whom he may desire to put in evidence for those of to-day and those of after-time to see and to understand how the winning of a wilderness to civilization affected the actors in the work, without living with them, sharing their toils, and making common interest with them in the affairs of their lives? He cannot, should he chance to meet the Simon-pure article and recognize him as such; while the chances of his taking false metal for good, and from its tawdry and pinchbeck character getting his ideas of color and texture and weight, are a thousand to one.

What Burns did for the Scotch peasant, he could do because, being one of them, living their life, his happy touch of genius not only could describe them as they seemed to themselves to be, but could, from similar life and like experiences, invest them with something that was in them, the capacity to bring something out of themselves, that reserve form or character of individualism which lends to written description the same fidelity and charm that the masters of old have with their brushes given to canvas.

A photograph is one thing; art makes quite another of the same subject.

The close intimacy which had of necessity sprung up between the two, gave Bud the desire of knowing more of what Zeb had done in the kind of life that to himself was so new; the more that, notwithstanding his apparent frankness, there was a reserve about the old man that had in it a savor of mystery; and with all the adroit turnings of the conversation he could manage, reënforced by some knowledge he had gained of his peculiarities, he sought to draw him out, sometimes with a temporary success, that led him to expect more again, and sometimes with no success at all. Still, many a tale of the hunt or of Indian skirmish or early days in California, strange happenings in the wilderness or Mexico, fell from Zeb's lips in those evenings. Under the excitement of narration, bits of his part in those happenings would unconsciously escape him, so modestly told, however, that only knowing the man, as Bud began to do, could he see the brave actor he had been in them all.

An occasional hunt by one or the other had, from time to time, added to their stock of elk and venison and filled the meat-house. Gradually the clouds began to thicken, and to Zeb's experienced eye, the shutting in of winter seemed close at hand.

"We'll have to take the hosses down," he said; "can't put it off much longer." As yet old Bally, his barometer, made no sign, but he watched him daily for indications.

They hastened the making of the snowshoes from the long pieces of wood they had brought into the cabin to dry, Zeb hewing the slabs down until they were rough boards five inches wide, a little over an inch thick, and nine feet long. "There's so much timber here," he said, "a short shoe will be better than twelve or fourteen feet ones, though they ain't so good where the ground favors."

Under his direction Bud finished them down, mainly with the knife, leaving them an inch thick at the middle and a little back of it, perhaps for a foot and a half, but paring the wood away from them to either end until it was hardly a quarter of an inch thick. What was to be the bottom was made as smooth as possible, and the front of each shoe was cut to a rounding point. The finishing touches old Zeb put on himself, from time to time, holding them up on one hand to get the proper balance. The pointed ends were then boiled or steamed, so that they might be curled up like sleigh-runners, and as only one could be heated at a time, the capacity of the lard can not being equal to more, it took some little time to heat them, and afterwards to bend them to the precise curve, in which constrained position they were left to dry until morning, and then tied down with fishlines to retain their shape.

An old pair of leather boot-legs were fished out from Zeb's "alfallcases" and cut into strips, which, being pinned to the sides of each shoe where the foot would come, made pockets for them. A little cross-piece was pinned far enough to catch the heel and help retain the foot in place; an extra smoothing was given to the bottom, and the shoes pronounced perfect.

Bud, with interest, watched their finishing, and, as he lifted one in his hands, expressed his fears that the shoes would prove too heavy.

"Why, Zeb," he said, "a man can't lift these things as they are, or with snow on them, and get along on them for half a mile."

"Ye don't lift 'em, Bud; ye slide them 'long like skates; we'll try 'em the first snow; ye must get a little savvy of 'em, for by the time we take out the hosses, or when we come back after leaving them, chances are we'll want 'em."

The next few days enough snow fell for practice, and under Zeb's tuition Bud acquired the sliding motion and began to think it would be easy to walk all day with them, and so said to his friend.

"'Tain't so easy as ye think," was the reply. "When the snow lies deep and its new snow, then one end will go up and the other will go down, and both of 'em want to go differnt ways, and they'll git covered with snow, and it will stick to the bottoms, and each one on 'em will weigh fifty pounds, and ye'll be that worn out and tired ye'll wish ye were dead; for days afterwards yer legs and yer back will ache, and ye'll be that stiff ye won't be no good; ye'll get uster 'em, though, and ye'll do right smart now.

"When we get back from taking the hosses down,

if the snow falls, as it's likely, I won't bring it up to ye that ye said 'twould be easy to snowshoe all day; 'twould be like Miss Pope, my old aunt, who'd always be a-throwing up to ye something ye had said, and doing it at some such time as that'll be.

"How cussed mad old man Pope uster get. He'd swear a blue streak, and he a deacon in the Church, and then he'd get right down and pray, a-stopping of his ears with his fingers; but 'twas nuts for us boys, yer bet yer."

Over a foot of snow had fallen, and Bally began to dislike the looks of the weather. His instinct told him it was time to get into winter quarters, and one morning, in a driving snow-storm, they started down the river with the horses. Their provisions for the trip—grub, more correctly speaking in the vernacular of the country—their guns, a blanket apiece, together with the two pairs of snowshoes, they could put on a pack-saddle on one of the animals, and so get them down easily, but evidently they would be something of a weight coming back; they would *caché* the pack-saddle where they left the horses, but their riding-saddles they did not dare to trust out so long, exposed to the winter and to the gnawing of the leather by any hungry animals who might take a fancy to them, and they could ride bare-back if they wished, and the way allowed.

"I wish we'd started yesterday," said Zeb; "there's that cañon to go down; we'll have to climb up pretty high to get along at all, and the snow's deeper than I wish it was, and she's a-coming faster and faster."

They soon found the way was more difficult than they had looked for, for the cañon through which the Salmon penetrates a country almost impassable in summer, is itself impossible of passage; and only by keeping high up on the craggy mountain sides can, even in the season most favorable, the descent of the river be made.

The snow, which along the stream was not over a foot and a half, grew deeper with every foot of altitude. To get to the winter range they had selected for the horses (a somewhat indefinite and uncertain range it was, for they had never seen it, and knew absolutely nothing about it, but Zeb's acquaintance with a mountain country made it certain to him that a low country of plain and rolling hill, where the snowfall would be light and the grass good, lay down the river within forty miles or so, and so they spoke of it as something that was) involved getting through or over the rim of mountains that enclosed the basin.

The impassable cañon required them to keep high up the mountain side, where the snow was heaviest, and the very ragged and broken character of the ground necessitated winding up and down to avoid obstacles of craggy rocks or dense timber or sharp declivities.

Sometimes they could ride a bit, only perhaps to fairly get on their horses when the impediments of snow, timber, or rock forced them to get off and exert all their strength to get themselves and the horses along.

They floundered on, often waist deep in snow, but made little progress in the direction they must go, owing to the zigzag course they had to take and the obstacles they encountered. Night came on, and they had not reached the divide in the pass. The fast falling snow made the way most difficult, and by morning it might be impassable.

Though horses and men were much fatigued, Zeb decided that they must press on, the only hope for the animals being to get them the other side of the divide as soon as possible. They made coffee, lighting a fire with difficulty, and while this was going on and the coffee was being drunk, the horses had a rest.

The storm was increasing, and there were still several miles to go before the divide could be reached. The river was below them, there was no doubt of their being able to keep their course; they had only to keep the hillside as they best could, and go as nearly in the course of the river as they might.

The pack was placed on a fresh horse, and all ranged in single file, old Bally leading, he being the steadiest to break trail after Zeb, who went ahead; Bud bringing up the rear, they started again.

To recount the struggles and toil of that weary walk would convey to the ordinary reader little idea of what they really were. A horse would get down, and, exhausted by his plungings, lie where he fell; he would have to be lifted on his feet, and the snow trampled down before him. One would stray down hill and with infinite labor in pushing and hauling, be brought back into line. Strength of body in both men and animals became quite exhausted, and only that power above physical strength, the power of will, kept them moving, the men urging on the weary animals and trampling the snow before them. Old Bally, who, from long companionship with his master, had imbibed something of his dogged perseverance and determination, kept his place behind Zeb, until, from sheer fatigue, the old fellow would fall on his knees; then the last horse in the line would be forced into his place and he put in the rear; the others, in their passage through the snow, making it easier going for him. Bud would take Zeb's place for a time, but, though a strong young man, he had not the seasoned sinews of the elder, and would soon become worn out, and Zeb would go to the front again. The instincts of the horses told them that sure death was behind them and a possibility ahead, and it was pitiable to see them stagger a few steps, stop, and then forge on again.

The steam, rising from the animals and the clothing of the men, caused by their violent exertion and the melting on them of the snow, now falling faster than ever, made them as wet as if they had been in the river below, and hung over them in the heavy air like a cloud, which in the dim light gave a weird appearance to the little cavalcade, increased by the silence, for no word was spoken and only the soft rustle of the snow as they ploughed their weary way through it, and an occasional snort from a horse, dispelled the illusion that this was some ghostly procession of storm spirits who, surrounded by the slightly luminous cloud, from time immemorial the accepted atmosphere of beings of the other world, were on their nightly travels.

I say no word was spoken, and none had been for some time. The horses, as they fell, were pushed on their feet again; the men took each other's place in the lead and fell behind again, and both would crawl back on hands and knees to bring up the rear when some animal had to be urged on.

At last it seemed impossible to get Bally on. He

had fallen with his neck and head extended, and his trembling body and half-closed eyes showed the old horse was near the limit of his power to move. To him had fallen the heaviest of the work of trail maker, and his sturdy frame, overtasked in his prodigious exertions, refused longer to continue the fight for life instinct told him was necessary.

Zeb took his head in his arms as he would have taken a child. "Bally, old man, Bally," he said, with tears in his voice, it was so tender and so soft, "ye musn't leave me, now. Steady, old cuss, steady, and we'll make it yet. Here, Bud, come and we'll lift him up;" but Bud had sunk down in the snow. Rousing him at last, they tried to get the old horse up, who with his feeble strength tried to help himself. Zeb arranged his legs under him, Bally whined plaintively as he did it, and then both men tried to raise him, but to no purpose. Zeb then tramped out the snow underneath him, and placing his feet on as solid bottom as he could beneath him, and getting his broad back well under the horse's side, with great effort and Bud's less efficient assistance, raised him a few inches. He sustained the weight while he took breath, and then throwing all his great strength into a last attempt, his hands on his knees, his long limbs rigid, he strained every muscle to its utmost, and with Bud's now more vigorous and better directed aid, the old horse trying to help himself, Bally was put on his feet again, and with many strokings and endearing words, and holding him up to steady him, was so far encouraged and strengthened as to warrant another start. But other horses were down and refused to rise, and the wearied men struggled with them until all were up.

For over twenty-four hours not a breath of wind had there been to give a slant to the snow, that, straight as a plumb-line, had been incessantly falling, but now came a little puff, and, as it came, Bally's nostrils dilated, and a glad snort, answered by each horse, told in plain words that something had revived their spirits.

"Thank God, the divide ain't far; Old Bally scents lower ground," said Zeb. "We're all right now; come on, old cuss," as, after having put two other horses ahead of him, Zeb trampled down the snow before them. They made another start. Every step increased the spirits of the horses; hope, that potent stimulant, made their sluggish blood flow again; responsive to it their muscles moved and they ploughed through the snow, now deeper than ever, with marvellous increase of strength and courage.

The men felt the impulse and pressed on with renewed vigor, having all they could do to keep out of the way of the animals who plunged after them.

At last they reached the divide and stopped for breath. "We must get 'em down the hill a couple of miles or so, as far as we can," said Zeb, "for we'll all be dang'd stiff after a rest."

Morning was just breaking, and save that there was a little wind, the storm showed no change. The driving snow did not allow of their seeing a hundred feet ahead, but of course their way was as plain as ever; they had but to go down hill, no more continued climbing, and with every foot of descent the snow would be getting lighter.

They started, and now, instead of having to laboriously lift the dead weight of their bodies, that very weight gave impetus to their descent, and plunging, ploughing, and tumbling through the snow, other muscles than those they had so long and tediously employed in their ascent being called into play, they moved with comparative comfort.

Nevertheless, by the time they reached a little flat—a small swag or gulch there opening out as it joined a large creek that continued on its way to the river, and some three miles from the divide—their strength failed, and horses and men sank down exhausted.

After a great struggle, trying nerve and strength to the utmost, when, after almost despairing, hope comes and gives us the vigor to succeed, like any other stimulant, its effect is temporary, passing away when the end is attained, and leaving us weaker from the expenditure of a reserve mental force. This once gone, we are not only at the end of our rope, so to speak, but, in the further extending of our limit, we have increased the weariness that before seemed all human nature could endure.

To men and horses had now come this reaction. The horses were down, Bud lay stretched in the snow asleep, and even the iron, or, rather, the steel, frame of old Zeb was fast getting under the dominion of his sleepy brain.

"This ain't going to do, Bud. Oh, Bud, git up and bring some dry wood and start a fire while I unpack and do something; ye can't go to sleep now;" and shaking him without effect, he rubbed Bud's face with snow, pulling him on his feet, and cuffing his face and ears. "Git up, I tell ye. We'll make a fire, git some grub into us, and we'll make a bed and take a sleep. I'm dang'd dull myself."

Half dazed, Bud stumbled about, and after a fashion managed to help Zeb take the light pack from the horse.

The tall rye grass in the little flat stood above the snow, which was now hardly two feet deep, and the horses roused themselves, and in a tired way nibbled at it, and the fire was made and the coffee and bacon cooked; bread they had brought with them.

The coffee and the food revived Bud and refreshed his wiry old companion. The fire had melted its way to the ground. A spot was cleared near it, the snow-shoes being used as shovels to remove the snow, fir-boughs were cut and thrown on the wet ground and made the bed. The blankets were spread, and wrapped in them the two went to sleep. The wind was blowing and the snow still coming fast, but in a minute both were unconscious.

It still wanted some hours of dark when Zeb awoke and piled fresh wood on the fire. Two or three inches of snow lay on the blankets, but the storm seemed nearly spent. The horses had made up to the fire, and, moving about it, showed an impatience to be off.

Bud was with difficulty aroused, and shivered over the fire, for his wet clothing made a turnout from bed anything but comfortable. The snow was shaken from the blankets, and they were held before the fire to dry, and then all was packed on Bud's pack-horse; the march was taken up again, Zeb walking, but Bud, too sore and lame at first to hardly move, was helped on his horse by Zeb, and rode, until either shame at seeing the old man sturdily striding down the hill, or the discomfort of bare-back riding, brought him to his feet, on which he staggered along in the rear.

They worked down stream a few miles, getting quite near the river, which, through lower hills or broken ground, was now making its way to a more level country, and in a fitting place made camp for the night.

The next night they reached what seemed to be a most desirable winter range, and concluded to go no farther, but leave the horses there, free to wander down stream should weather or inclination prompt them. In a tree they *cachéd* the pack-saddle, taking a mental note of its position; they congratulated themselves on the prospect of abundant feed, water, and shelter the range afforded.

The horses, when turned out, fell to eating the grass with appetites that fasting and fatigue had made most keen.

"I'm pretty well beat out," Bud said that evening. "I thought I could hold my own with most any man; but you are fresh, and I'm sore and lame and tired all over."

"Well, Bud, yer young and soft and green. I've been doing this sort of thing, or something like it, for forty years, and I've got tough and hard. We'll camp another day here 'fore we start back; ye'll git limber soon, and we won't have no such pull as we had. I was nigh done up myself 'fore we got to the divide, when old Bally came so clost to giving out."

The storm cleared with cold, freezing weather. A rousing fire, with a great stick for a back log, helped out the protection given by the two blankets making their bed; and with their feet to the heat, they managed, by replenishing the fire at times, to keep warm. Their fatigue induced sleep, and, spite of the cold, they were greatly refreshed next morning.

That day was spent looking after the horses, and by going about, further satisfying themselves that the range would be safe and comfortable for the horses until spring.

With much fondling and many injunctions "to take care of yourself, old cuss," and whinnyings from old Bally, Zeb and he took leave of each other.

While in many respects Bally was by temperament utterly vicious, and unmanageable by any one but his master, biting and kicking at Bud on the slightest attempt at familiarity, obstinate and perverse, his affection for Zeb was an overmastering passion with him, and on this last evening he came up to the fire, standing for minutes watching his friend, and when the tenderness in his crabbed old heart could no longer restrain itself, he would go up to him and put his head on his shoulder, Zeb talking to him meanwhile.

"Dog gone ye, Bally, I hate to leave ye, but ye see here's grass and water and little snow, and ye'll have a good time this winter, and we'll both come out fat in the spring. Dang yer old heart, but it's too bad! Keep out from behind him, Bud; he's an old devil. Yes, yer a bad one, Bally, but ye love me, don't ye?" as the horse would lick his ear and face. "Yer a-kissing of me. Nobody knows ye but me. Kissing me, a-kicking and a-rearing up and biting at everybody else. Well, it ain't for me to say nothing; but an old cuss like ye oughter to have better manners. Why, old man, 'pears like yer thought ye'd never see me again. Here's salt for ye, and when ye eat that, clear out and feed; ye have your business and I've got mine."

Notwithstanding this command, Bally lingered about the fire, watching them as they ate, edging himself up to Zeb, and resting his head against him. "What's inter ye, Bally? Yes," as the horse would whinny, "it's too bad, too dang bad! But I'll come for ye when the grass is green."

Not until their first pipes were smoked did Bally, with a last putting down of his head to his master's face, as he found chance to do between the puffs of smoke, and many a fond caress in return, move hesitatingly away, stopping and turning back his head as he went.

"The old cuss knows we're going to leave, and something is on his mind more nor common; he ain't more nor seventeen year old, and he's sound as a dollar. He can't git no harm here. I never see a better place to winter stock, but it makes me feel bad the way he acts, he's so dang wise. I hope nothing will happen to him; 'twould knock me out, we've been friends so long. 'Tain't a Christian thing to say, but I'd rather see some men die than him. He's onery, I know; a onery old devil, if there ever was one; but we're friends. He don't vally any one else a tinker's dam; he's took to me."

"I never could make friends with him," said Bud.

"No, nor no one else. I never see sich a hoss. There's a good deal of dog about him, only dogs ain't so bad. A good dog don't want to have nobody a-patting him and a-talking to him but his master, but he'll give anybody a civil answer and put up with a heap, cause a dog's naterally polite; but Bally, he's the worst I ever see. Never would make up with nobody but me, and always got mad if anybody else spoke to him or looked at him."

"How long have you had him, Zeb?"

"Well, let's see; mebbe twelve years or so. I was in the Grande Ronde Valley, and I passed some fellers with a band of hosses. I see Bally in among 'em, and I took a notion to him. A feller stumped me to trade for a mule I had, and said: 'I'll give ye yer pick of the band and ten dollars for that mule;' good mule he was, but I hadn't had him long and didn't care nothing 'special 'bout him.

"'That's a go,' said I, and I picked Bally out of the band. I see from the feller's talk that something was wrong with him. He said he'd rather I had taken any other hoss and all that, but I had sized them hoss men years afore, and I knew that something was wrong with the hoss. They're deceiving men—all hoss-traders is—and I didn't like the way he was talking, trying to make me keen to take Bally, but I was in for it, and I said, 'That's the one I want.'

"After a while he and another man with him caught up the hoss, Bally rareing up and kicking, and biting at the lariat they threw on his neck, and yer couldn't git nigh him, so they had to lass him by the hind foot and throw him. We got my rope on him at last, and they rode off with the mule, and me a-holding Bally. He'd pull back on the rope and kick and rare and yell, and then he'd come up and try to strike me with his fore-feet, squealing and bawling all the time.

"I was a better man then than I be now, but I had as hard a tussle with that hoss as I ever had in my life. First off I'd a-sold him for two bits, and then I'd have given a man a twenty-dollar piece to take him off my hands, and then I come down to business. No man could buy that hoss for no money. 'Dang ye,' says I, 'yer my hoss, and I hain't yer man by a plaguey sight!' I held onto the rope, and when he'd come up to strike at me, I'd knock him in the head with my fist and stagger him. The rope I had on him was stout. I'd always been a-cussing at that rope, it was so big and heavy. But, so it goes; ye'll cuss a thing for all that's out, and first thing yer know 'twill come in as handy as a pocket in a shirt; it was just the thing then, ye bet. I got the end of the rope snubbed round a tree, and at last I brought him up short to it. I was that tuckered I sat down and looked at Bally. I never see sich a wicked eye in a hoss before. He was a-kicking and rareing and a-rolling on the ground, and then he'd brace himself and set back on his legs and pull on the rope, but the rope was stout and he couldn't budge it.

"I unpacked and camped right there, for water and grass was handy.

"I ain't no hoss man, never was, and always despised a kicking, bucking cayuse, and here I'd been and got the meanest hoss a man ever had; but my blood was up and I was going to master him if I killed him or he killed me.

"That night I thought it all over, and the next morning I tackled him. I'd kept him without a bite to eat, for I'd drawn him up so clost to the tree he couldn't git his head down; but when I went up to him, he was just fierce as ever, biting at me and squealing with madness. 'Oh, ye devil,' I said, 'I'll take this out of ye.' I hain't no man to 'buse a hoss nor nothing that walks; but that hoss was a-going to git sense or he was going to die. I warn't in no hurry; I got something to eat and smoked. I thought I'd keep him another day without eating or drinking, and mebbe 'twould tame him; but I hadn't nothing to do only to look at him, and he looked so wicked and it seemed kinder mean to fight anything when it was weak from hunger and thirst, and I thought I'd give the cuss some show.

"There was alders along the crick, and I cut a good one nearly three inches thick, and six foot, or so, long. I went up to the hoss with my club in my hand, and let out the rope, so that he had twenty feet of it to circle round with. As soon as he had this liberty he made for me, his eye as wicked as ever, and rareing up he tried to strike me with both his front feet. I watched my chance and hit him in the head with my club—a terrible blow it was, for the alder was strong and heavy—and he fell like a log. I thought I'd killed him, and I went up to him, but he was only stunned; and while I was a-talking kind to him, he got on his feet, looking kind of dazed like. Pretty soon the devil came in him again, and he rushed at me, and I knocked him down again; and then I thought I had surely killed him, he lay so long; but at last, all of a tremble, he got up and looked at me. We looked each other steady in the eye for a bit, and then his eyes dropped and I knew I had him.

"I picketed him on good grass after giving him some water, but he wouldn't feed, though he drank well. All that day he didn't eat, and would watch me, not like he was afeared, but like he was a-thinking.

"That night I heerd him a-feeding, and the next

morning I went up to him like all had been friendly between us. He let me pat him after a while, and I give him some salt. He let me put a pack on him; the one I had taken off the mule when we traded. 'Twas all new to him, and he didn't like it. The devil would get in his eyes again, and I would look him hard and strong, and his eyes would drop, but I led him that day 'bout six miles, and he was like any young hoss with his first load on, but quieter. He would let me handle him and was a-watching me all the time. I was kind to him and talked to him. That night I picketed him with the other two hosses I had. Next morning I packed him again, and was a-kneeling down, cutting a string from a buckskin, when I heerd him snap a little rope he was tied with and come a-charging for me. My gun was on the ground near me, and I got up with it just as his front feet missed me. I brought the gun down on his head and knocked him stiff, but that gun was no good no more.

"I never struck Bally again, not even with a switch. When he come to I got him up, spoke kind to him, and stroked his head. 'Twas a long time afore we got down to be real friendly, but we did, and no better hoss no man ever had than him. We've had tough times and we've had easy times, but Bally's been there all the time. I could tell ye things that old hoss has done would surprise ye. Most men wouldn't believe me, but they'd be gospel truth. Since you saw me, I've been a-packing him, 'cause that gray of mine hain't no sense with a pack; hangs himself on every tree he comes to, so I have to ride him, but Bally is my riding hoss, and better no man's got for rough work.

"'Twas in '77, or thereabouts, I was south of Snake River and the Injuns was bad. I was a-goin' from Silver down to Goose Crick way, where I had left a pack hoss and some traps, only me and Bally. I had my gun, a little grub, and a blankit; riding light like. I hadn't seen no Injuns, and while they was on my mind, there wan't no sign. Still, I made fire one day, 'bout three hours sundown, cooked, and then rode on eight miles or so, and camped. I let Bally loose and lay down to sleep. Just 'bout light I woke by him a-biting and pulling the blankit. I knew something was up, for he has a naterel savey of Injuns, and hates 'em like the devil. I got up and saddled as still as I could. I had to cross a fork of the Bruneau, not more nor half a mile or so from where I camped. I rode down towards the ford. It was full light when we got nigh the ford, for I had picked along, keeping the high ground as much as I could. I didn't like Bally's actions; he was a-snorting and a-winking of his ears. The ford was in a place where it was open and clear of bushes, and just before I got there a couple of shots come and the bullets whistled by me. Being as the ground near the ford was so open, I made to cross the river below it, and into the water we went, slap into a hole that took Bally off his feet, and he tuck on't swimming. I didn't want to wind the hoss there, for the stream was high and rough, with a surgin' current, so I slipped off the saddle, and keeping my gun high, paddled 'long side of the hoss. Just as we got to the other bank, and where it was steep and hard to git up, the shots come in putty fast, one of 'em ploughing along Bally's shoulder and one on 'em barking my neck here," as he put his hand up, where was an old scar, one of the many that his head and face bore, and indicated the place. "We got up the bank somehow, but Bally broke away from me and run off. I had got to trust him and it hurt me, but I went into the willows, going along as fast as I could, when, as I'm a live man, I see Bally coming back to me. He came up and turned, and waited for me to get on him; I jumped into the saddle, and we were off like scat. Bally under me and Injuns behind I was all right, for no Injun could catch us, I knew that dang well, so I monkeyed along. After a bit some on 'em followed, but I nailed one devil. I saw him throw up his hands when he was struck, Injun like, and I plugged another, but I misdoubt killing him, and then Bally showed his heels to the whole outfit. That's how that white streak come along his shoulder. Well, after that, I set a heap on that hoss, and I've other reasons for it, too.

"But dang it, since I met ye, Bud, I'm a-telling things I had forgot. Somehow things come to me, and one brings on another when we get a-talking. We'd better make an early start to-morrow, so let's turn in."

CHAPTER VI

CARRYING their snowshoes and blankets, which, with their guns, somewhat encumbered their movements, they started back before sunrise next day. The rising ground on their way gave them a sight of the horses feeding in the level below.

"Good luck to ye, Bally," said Zeb; "I hope ye'll winter well, but I ain't that easy in leaving ye. I wish I was. But ye'll be all right, I know ye will. Dog gone a cussed country where a man can't keep his hoss with him six months in the year. I swear every winter that the next one I'll be out of the snow, but I'm that dang fool, winter comes and snow comes, and I'm third man every time."

Late in the afternoon the snow became deeper, making it easier to walk on the shoes than to carry them. They made a few miles with them, Bud adding to his knowledge of the art.

"Camp's but twenty miles from here, I reckon. We must have come eighteen miles to-day, and I don't think it's more nor thirty-eight miles from the cabin to where we left the hosses," said Zeb, around the fire in the evening.

"We'll be in camp by this time to-morrow night, then?"

"Mebbe we will, but ye'll find it quite a pull, I tell ye. The snow hasn't packed much. and 'twill be slow work from this on. Ye'll be kind of sore tomorrow morning from this little walk to-day, and ye'll be more 'fore we get front of the fireplace, Bud."

Youth has faith of its own, that knowledge of things unseen, the foundation of hope, for hope belongs to youth, but the wisdom of one day is the folly of the next. Bud knew he could make the cabin easily the next day, but when the day came, it was hardly noon before he changed his mind. Zeb had gone on slowly, stopping frequently to give the young man breath; for himself, he could have made twice the distance in the time.

As they came to one of these pauses, Bud said, "I'm going to carry my shoes a while; this slipping along and pushing the weight of them is tiresome."

"Give me the shoes," Zeb insisted; "ye'll find it all ye want to carry yerself in this snow."

And he soon found it was, and got on the shoes again, but after a little he suggested that they stop and take their lunch. After this and a smoke, and as long a rest as Zeb would allow, they took up the march again.

Laboriously Bud toiled, his shoes getting heavier with every step, and the way growing steeper. His back ached, the muscles of his legs were sore, and his ankles were tired and worn from the effort of keeping the shoes straight, but he kept grittily on for an hour or two, until Zeb saw he was fast fagging out.

"We'll go on half a mile or so and make camp," he said; "there's a good place there, and to-morrow we can make it in, it ain't more nor twelve miles or so now."

Next day Bud could hardly rise. Their insufficient bed-clothing had, in spite of the fire, kept him cold all night, and he began the last day's walk in sorry plight, dragging along his legs with pain and difficulty.

To get to the summit, a sharp pitch of a mile or so had to be ascended. Sometimes on his shoes; sometimes wading in the snow, carrying them; sometimes on hands and knees, with great toil and pain, he at last gained Zeb on the ridge, who, carrying the blankets, had gone ahead.

His progress had been so slow that two hours had been spent in making the last mile, and he was, as he told Zeb, "about dead."

"It's mostly down hill from here on; there's no sharp rise, anyway. Get your breath and rest a little. All ye'll have to do will be to keep on yer shoes. Take the stick and poke along with it, and when ye git going too fast put it between yer legs, and let the end drag in the snow behind. Ye can sit down on it, and it's like a rough lock on a wheel or a brake. Don't let the shoes run away with ye, mind that," said Zeb.

Going down hill is naturally easier than going up; for an object lesson to clearly demonstrate this proposition, snowshoeing on the long or Norwegian shoe has no equal. You have, with the greatest exertion, on the level, or, worse still, up hill, pushed your shoes, clogged and heavy with snow, slipping back if the ground allows, hanging behind of their own weight, getting heavier and more unmanageable, and you come to a descent. Life begins in the dead, inert shoes; they glide along without a movement on your part; they are carrying you, instead of your carrying them. On they go; all you have to do is to stand up on them and direct their course. If the descent is steep and the run long, they start, gliding so smoothly, increasing their speed every minute; they go over some little inequality with a bound; they clear some larger thing with a jump; they are running along like a locomotive; they dart like the flight of a fool hen; they overcome distance like a rifle ball; no longer inanimate, wooden clogs that with strained muscles you have tediously been urging on, but living things, tearing along in mad exuberance of spirit, madder and madder as the pace grows hotter.

You may have ridden a mettlesome horse on some cool autumn morning. You have given him rein; he trots, he gallops, he leaps; as his blood gets warmer an intoxication comes over him; the champagne of the frosty air goes to his head; he takes the bit in his mouth; faster and faster he goes over wood and water, like a thistle-down blown by the wind.

We will say you are a cool, phlegmatic kind of a man; even if you are, you slowly begin to feel the wine acting on you, and gradually you partake of the good steed's exhilaration. Your blood comes and goes; to every bound of the horse your ecstatic spirit, your body, lifts itself; so light you feel yourself, 'tis thistle-down on thistle-down; and if you be of those who feel they can ride as fast as a horse can run, that union of horse and man comes to you.

You may love a dog. His affection for you, his simple, untiring devotion to and absorption in you, makes him, of all animals, the only true friend man has, but you are none of him nor he of you. You are distinct individuals, necessary to each other, each complementing the other; but there are times when a good horse is part of you and you of him. To no other animal comes this union with man. Is it a mere physical phenomenon bred of rushing through air together with a common object and in a common spirit; or has, in the evolution of both from the one germ cell, something common to each clung to them-through all the varying phases of their diverse development? However that may be, the subject is too abstruse for us here. If you are a horseman, you will recognize the fact, whatever be the cause; if you are not, or only know a horse as an animal to drag wheels over a good road, your only communication with him being through long lines of leather, all this may seem far-fetched.

On the long Norwegian snowshoes, down a hill, there is much to remind you of what I hope you have sometimes felt on a horse; but to a novice with either there often comes a sudden check, and so it was with Bud. He had with pleasure experienced the grateful sensation of riding on his shoes, as feeling the downward grade they slid along; and to resist their evident intention of one going one way and the other straight on, or turning still another way, he had from time to time used his pole to break their speed; but as confidence came to him, and they seemed to run more truly, he allowed them more freedom.

Going down a little incline with a rush that quite suited him, for he was by nature of a stirring habit, and getting a little knack of holding them in their proper relative positions, observing, too, how easily their motion was checked when the incline became less steep, he grew overconfident of his powers of control of them, and allowed them to attain quite a degree of speed, and hardly noticed that they had gotten on a long steep incline and were beginning to run with him. In trying to get his pole between his legs to add his weight to retard them with that brake, he lost his pole and with it all control of the shoes.

Faster and faster they went, the trees whizzing by him as he sped on. They had taken the bit in their teeth, and were carrying him in the wildest run he had ever made. He tried to keep his legs rigid; he thought of falling down, but there seemed no good place to do it and avoid being dashed against the trees. He seemed going to inevitable destruction with the swiftness of a cannon ball.

Absolute paralysis seized him, and he only awaited an end that in a few seconds or minutes he felt must come to him, when he would be dashed to death against some great tree trunk.

Fortunately, however, fate had reserved Bud for other things; and one shoe striking a twig so as to deflect its course, and the other going straight ahead, he was hurled twenty feet through the air and buried in the snow, where Zeb, who had been passed in his wild flight, found him unconscious, and after vigorously rubbing his face with snow finally brought him to.

"Ye'll be a better snowshoer afore ye make two miles in that time again, I bet ye, Bud. Why didn't ye sit down or fall off or do something? It's God's mercy and a fool's luck ye warn't killed. Yer all right; no bones broken," said Zeb.

Bud's gun had been strapped behind his back, Zeb, on account of his superiority on the shoes, having insisted on carrying all the load. Besides a general shaking up, he had a great bruise across his head, made by the gun-barrel when he fell, but no serious injury had been received; and after Zeb had collected the shoes, which had brought up against some bushes whose tops stood above the snow, Bud, weak and still dazed by his fall, was able to proceed.

It was well along in the night before the friendly shelter of the cabin was reached, and only Zeb's assistance and support got them there then.

For many days Bud felt the effects of his first snow-shoe trip, and it was three before he could join Zeb at their work. Every bone he had ached, every muscle was sore, but Zeb never alluded to his friend's confidence in his ability to snowshoe.

Other storms came, and it took half their time to shovel the snow away to clear the cut, but in spite of all this they made good progress.

Every day they took a pan of gravel, sometimes two or three pans, and washed it; they could no longer doubt but that they had really "struck it." Sometimes they would get of gold, what Zeb would call "a bit to the pan." Sometimes it would be five cents, or ten cents, sometimes only a cent; and once they panned through a streak that produced five bits in each of several pans. All these grains of gold were carefully secured, and the little phial Zeb put them in was nearly half full, and had perceptible weight; he thought over an ounce.

The storms had driven away the deer and elk, and the bear had holed up; a lynx now and then, the pine martens in the trees, a few cotton-tail rabbits, and, judging from the tracks, an occasional cougar and wolverine, were, with the few winter birds, the only dwellers in Yellow Pine Basin, save Zeb and Bud.

Certainly there was no human being within a hundred miles, unless somewhere in the wilderness a trapper might be plying his lonely avocation.

A round of hard labor during the hours of light, which now, short as was the distance, they went to and from on their snowshoes, filled in the days. Bud became quite expert in the management of the snowshoes, for besides running on them every day a little, they would on Sundays take long walks up hill and down, making runs down all the steep pitches they found. He acquired the slide, and Zeb assured him he would make a good snowshoer, for his strength and wind needed only practice to make him as good as the best. Zeb even told him he might get to be as good a man on shoes as was "snowshoe Thompson," these many years the ideal of those who in the far Western snows practise the art in which he was so proficient.

It was well along in December, near Christmas, and there came great storms, the snow falling steadily for days. At last it seemed labor lost to shovel out the cut every morning, and the day before Christmas they decided to stop work until the storm should cease. Bud had killed a couple of rabbits, and they were to have a Christmas dinner worthy of the day.

"I'll get the dinner," said Zeb, "and mind ye, I don't want ye monkeying around the fire. When a man's cooking common grub he don't care, but when he's got anything on his mind like this yer dinner, he don't want nobody chipping in. Yank uster say I could make a rabbit stew better nor any one, and for duffs he said I lay over 'em all. When he'd get a little too much (we was young then, Bud), he was always talking 'bout me, and if anybody said anything the least agin me, he'd fight and raise the devil, and nobody could do nothing with him but me. He was a terror, Yank was, and 'twas his rule to get drunk on Fourth of July and Christmas. 'Whatever I am,' he uster say, 'I'm an American and a Christian, and I'll observe them days.'

"He uster feel so good them mornings when he'd go out of the cabin and make a bee line for a saloon. He had an idee 'twas his duty; and when Yank thought he had a duty on hand, he didn't hang back, that warn't his way; but he'd smile like, and go to it as peart as you please. Didn't make no difference what it was, nor how bad, nor how good, it was all the same; and so he had that idee 'bout them days. Curous, warn't it? I never had no like for getting drunk—course I did sometimes—but I hadn't no taste that way. But when it come Fourth of July I had to, that's all. Yank would have it so, but Christmas he warn't so sot on.

"'What pious ideas you has, Zeb,' he uster say, 'is naterally Baptist, and there's a kind of water streak in 'em. Bein' raised that way, your idees is differnt; but there ain't but one idee 'bout Fourth of July. Yer an American and it's Fourth of July.' And so I jist had to git drunk; he wouldn't have it no other way.

"Well, one Christmas, long say '55 or so, I said I'd make a duff; and Yank says, 'I'll go down and obsarve the day like a Christian.' That was a dig at me, for Yank had a low-down idee of Baptists; but I didn't care, nor, for the matter of that, did Yank either. I had raisins and citron and brandy—I wish to Lord I had some now and I'd show ye a duff to-morrow—and I made the slickest duff I ever did make that day; it was a posey.

"Dinner-time come, and I took out the duff, for, drunk or sober, Yank was always on time. He prided himself on that. I put it on the table, and I never see no such duff before nor sence. I heerd a noise and went to the door, and there was Yank coming up the gulch with his gun drawn on a black-haired, black-whiskered, wicked-looking Spaniard, and a crowd a-followin' 'em. In Yank marched him. 'Dog gone ye,' he says, 'Zeb can't make a duff fit for a hog to eat, can't he? Sit ye down there and eat that duff, or I'll blow yer head off.' And as I'm a living man he made the Spaniard eat the whole duff; 'twas hot and 'twas big. He liked to burn himself and bust himself, and the last of it went hard, too.

"I tried hard to stop Yank. 'Why, Zeb,' he says, 'the Greaser has said things of ye no man shall say. Drive on,' he'd say, as the man would stop while I was talking; 'bolt that ere duff or yer a dead man;' and the crowd that would come with 'em was a-laffin'. When it was all down the man, Yank catches him by the collar and kicks him out, and then he laffed fit to kill, and asked the crowd to go down and take a drink, and they all went off with him.

"Well, that's how that duff went. The way of it was this. Yank had filled himself up pretty well, and the Greaser come into the saloon, kinder looking for a fight, for he was one of them kind of fellers; folks was kinder shy of him, he'd shoot and he'd cut so; but Yank, drunk or sober, never feered nothing that walked. The Greaser was trying to bring on a fight, for he'd said in the other gulch what he'd do to Yank, but Yank was good natured, and never looked for no fight, and 'twas Christmas Day, and he warn't goin' to fight 'less he had to, and so they kinder kept apart. The saloon was full, for everybody knew Yank would take so much, and though he was peaceable, when he'd stood enough he'd fight. Yank was a-tellin' 'bout me, like he always did at them times, and he said I could make a better duff than any man in Californy; and the Greaser, seein' a p'int to chip in, said he lied, I couldn't make a duff fit for a hog to eat. That was enough for Yank, and he made for him with his fists, but the feller drew and missed. Yank was on him like a bulldog, took away his gun and drew his. 'Come along with me, ye dirty Greaser,' he says; 'come along with me;' and so he marched him up to the cabin and made him eat that duff, as I say.

"First off, I was mad at Yank, and then I laffed myself at the idee of the thing. I making that duff, the finest I ever did make, and Yank and me so fond of duff, and then his making that man eat it clean up so we didn't get a bit of it. That was Yank all over, though; he warn't like no other man I ever see.

"I said to him next morning, when he was sober, 'The next duff I make, I'll make for company.' 'What's that?' says he. 'Why, Zeb, that onery Greaser never had no duff before; now he knows what a duff is, and that you kin make a good one, and that was the p'int of the argyment.' Yank never liked me to speak 'bout that, though."

CHAPTER VII

Christmas Eve came, with the storm at its height; for three days the snow had been falling continuously, and the little cabin was nearly covered, and by morning threatened to be quite so.

But inside all was comfort. A big pile of wood had been cut and stacked up inside, a bright fire was burning in the fireplace, and its cheerful blaze illuminated the interior. On Zeb's chair was spread the great skin of the silver tip, it's broad head over the back, falling almost to the floor, it's great pads and long claws stretched out on either side. Bud's skin, glossy, and black as night, covered his seat, and both contributed to these mean and common pieces of furniture the dignity that attaches to rich fur, whether it be on a king's throne or on a log before a campfire.

The fireplace, on either side of which were these fur-covered chairs, was broad and deep and high; a great log, black, even a little charred, from the smoke and heat below, made a rough shelf over it.

The stones of which the fireplace was built were of irregular shapes and sizes, no attempt having been made to place them at all smoothly, and jutting out here and there at the sides and back, their darkened faces, with a thick layer of soot in places from the pitchy nature of the fuel used, gave the effect of a corner of an old stone fence over which a forest fire had swept, singeing and blackening the moss that had here and there been attached to its stones.

As the fire burnt, the falling snow made entrance through the wide chimney, and as it dropped on the heated coals, produced a singing sound like that from a boiling tea-kettle. On wooden pegs driven into the logs on each side hung the frying-pans; the old lard can and the coffee can, completing the cooking utensils of the cabin, standing on the hearthstone, at one side.

The dirt floor had by this time hardened, being twice a day moistened and neatly swept with a broom Zeb had made of willow twigs. In one corner were the saddles, bridles, old saddle-blankets, ropes, and other horse gear piled up in an orderly way. Against the wall was the table of Bud's manufacture, and on it the tin plates, cups, knives, forks, and spoons were arranged. Above it ran a long shelf hewn from a log and fastened to the wall with big wooden pins.

On this were tins of baking powder, packages of coffee, a bag of salt, a few boxes of cartridges, and many other smaller things. At the two corners most remote from the fire were two bunks made of poles, and over the bottom of them thick layers of rye grass, on which were the blankets; some old clothes at the head for pillows completed the beds. A Winchester resting on forked sticks, and dangling below it a cartridge-belt partly filled, hung over each bunk, and two small shelves near by held little odds and ends. Among these things on Zeb's shelf appeared a small brown-covered Testament, a particularly treasured thing it was, he often removing the dust from it with great care and no little tenderness, though it lay thickly enough and unmolested on his sewing-bag and some fish-lines and other things. Under one of the bunks were drills and hammers, a gold-pan, and such other articles as naturally gravitated to so convenient and retired a place of storage. The last remaining corner had in it the sacks in which was the stock of flour, fast decreasing, and over it hung what was left of the bacon; it had been very sparingly used, the deer and elk meat being in such plenty. The axe resting against the wood pile completed the contents of the cabin. The ruddy light from the fire, softening much that was rude and meagre, threw around an air of comfort, a sort of home look, over articles and surroundings, that, as I describe them, seem so rough and common. But on Christmas Eve a palace may be dreary in its splendor—a mountain log cabin cheery in its rudeness.

When we pass out of childhood we leave illusions whose memories, recurring to us as holidays come, give us an uncertain pleasure, tinged with a certain melancholy; our minds, in spite of us, go back to the times when life was young in us, and the world we have since found made up of so much shade and sunshine was all bright without a shadow.

With years come the experiences that leave gashes and ruts in our hearts. What we have gained and what we have lost strike a balance, and most of us find it heavily on the wrong side. The closer we keep to our childish faith, the simpler lives we lead, the less do we feel all this. Zeb was like a child in many ways, with a heart so kindly and so cheery that the demands he felt made on his good spirits by Christmas times he could easily respond to. Bud, not half his age, could not so readily come under the spirit of the time; there was so sharp a contrast between this Christmas Eve and others he had passed, that he was sad and moody. Many a cheerful remark of the old man could not dissipate his gloom.

"Bud, let me tell ye somethin'," he said. "There are some folks that, when they has the least show in the world, is always thinking about somethin' that's gone, or hain't gone to their notion, and the more miserable and onery the thing is, the more they think and gits to feel luck is agin 'em. If things had gone so and so, they'd be rich, or they'd be this or that.

"Did ye ever think what cussed foolishness that is, Bud? If a thing's gone, it's gone, vamoosed, that's the end on it; ye can't bring it back, and ten to one if ye could, ye'd be worse off than ye are. When a thing's gone, let it go. Ye'll hear a man say, 'If this one or that one had been eddicated, what a man he would be—President may be; or if he had some one to help, how rich he would be, and so on.' All foolishness. If ye got a head to be President, yer a-going to get the eddication. There was old Johnson; after he was married, his wife taught him his letters, but he got there, didn't he? And all the rich men I ever heer'd on made the riffle 'cause perhaps they was spryer on the trail after a dollar, or meaner or smarter, or somethin' else, than other men. I'm goin' to be old Zeb long as I live. Why? 'Cause it ain't in me to be nothing but old Zeb. I hope I'm squar, and I hope I'm white; and if I am, that's all I am or going to be. Yer a young man, Bud; I see p'ints in ye. Yer eddicated, and Lord knows what yer going to be, but ye'll be just what ye make yerself. There's no roads, there's no trails, there's no animals to carry ye into the time that's to come.

"Ye've just got to hoof it along yerself, and so be if ye've got the wind and the savvy, and don't get off on no blind trails, thinking ye see a road where they ain't none, ye'll make it. If yer kind of lame and spavined and foundered, and hain't got the right sense, ye'll be a-plugging 'long just as I am, just as I always will be, and if yer always a-thinking 'if I'd turned off here or gone that way or the other, I'd have been all right,' ye'll make yerself miserable when ye might be right peart and comfortable.

"There are some things happened to me, Bud, and for one thing I wish I was rich, God knows I do, 'cause I've got use for money. Ye wouldn't think it, Bud, but I has. Here I am, sixty come March. Ain't I healthy? I'm poor, but I hain't got no great weight on my conscience. I've got grub and a good cabin, and ain't I happy? Don't I feel good? I've got a good pardner and half of a good claim. That claim will make us money; I know 'twill, Bud, I know 'twill. And there ye are, young and strong and hearty, and ye've got a cabin and grub, and ye've got half of a good claim."

"Yes, Zeb, and the best partner a man ever had," said Bud, for there was no resisting Zeb's kind voice and his way.

"I'm going to do somethin', Bud. Yank always did it on a Christmas Eve, and I've seen it done at posts and in towns and in camp, and when I'm alone I always do it on Christmas Eve. I've done it with whiskey, and I've done it with only water, and I've done it with wine, and now I'm going to do it with tea; that's a woman's drink, and so it's right fit. I've got a little tea in my sewing-bag, I've been a-saving of it;" and the old man going up to his bag drew from it a little canvas pouch, and poured from it a little tea into his hand, and putting it into the coffee can after cleaning it, and heating some water in it, the brew was made.

"We ought to have sugar to put in it," he said, "but as we hain't none, we'll have to sweeten it from our hearts," as he poured the infusion into two tin cups, one for Bud and one for himself.

With something unusual in his firm, clear voice, he gave the old toast, "Sweethearts and wives, God bless 'em!" and the cups were drained. "Not that I've got any to count, but other men has, and I say again, God bless 'em!" he added.

Where men of English speech, on land or sea, up in the Arctics, along the Equator, in peril or in peace, were gathered away from home and those they loved, went up that night that same old toast, as for hundreds of years before it has gone, and God grant for hundreds of years yet it may go. It has risen amidst creaking of masts and snapping of cordage, death knocking at the door, with great waves of every sea that on a Christmas Eve has tossed our fathers.

With "the shouts of them that triumph, and the song of them that feast," with the wail of defeat, and amidst the pangs of famine, has the old toast had its place. "Sweethearts and wives, God bless them!" No more heartfelt prayer was ever made than those words have borne from the millions who have uttered them.

There was a touch of dignity in old Zeb's manner

as he did this, a fervidness in the spoken words that impressed Bud. It seemed to open to him something new in the old mountaineer. He had been struck at times before with some such feeling; but there was something in the way he gave the toast, something in his giving it at all, something in the tremor of his voice he had never heard quaver before, that was new to him and increased the desire he had long had to know more of this man, who evidently had a history.

Zeb was now quite in the mood for Christmas Eve; he was full of hearty mirth, and his mind and talk ran from Mexico to Alaska, and back to his childhood in Indiana, and how this and that Christmas was passed. He was sleigh-riding with the boys and girls, companions of his youth; he was at a fandango in Mexico; he was at a ball in Hangtown; and he related with great glee the story of a Christmas Eve with Yank at the "Bay," as San Francisco is called by the old timers.

The old fellow took great pleasure in getting off his "Merry Christmas" to Bud next morning, long before light, and in a voice that nearly lifted the roof and awoke his partner. The Christmas dinner was a grand success, and the duff was, Bud declared, the best he ever ate.

The storm that had already raged so long was yet furious, and the snow, piling up fast, was well up on the roof of the little cabin. It was no easy thing to shovel out the spring to get water, or to replenish the supply of wood. But dinner was over, and wood and water in. As they sat before the fire, it's light shone brightly on a scar on Zeb's neck, and Bud asked him: "How did you get that scar, Zeb?"

"Bullit," said the old man.

"But where and how did you get it?"

"I got that down South, in the war. That one I got at Atlanty. I was in the war and was hit."

"Why, Zeb, how did you get East? I thought you were always out West here, until I heard you say something once before about the war."

CHAPTER VIII

"Well, 'twas this way. We uster have talk, Yank and me, 'bout slavery. Yank's idee was that a nigger was a man, and had a right to be free, and go where he pleased, and do what he liked, Constitution or no Constitution. The Constitution said all men was born free and equal, and a nigger was a man, and that was all there was 'bout it. Seemed reasonable, but I was no nigger lover, and would have said right out the Constitution says "all white men," but Yank warn't no man to mistell a thing; and though I thought it said all white men, I hadn't the nerve to say so, afeered I might be wrong; and course we was where we couldn't see no one of them maps that hang on the wall, picturs of the Presidents all around the edges, and the Constitution printed in the middle.

"We was in Nevady, 'bout forty miles from Reese River, in the winter of '60 and '61, and had a quartz claim there, and was puttin' in the winter sinking a shaft. We got hold of two or three old papers that winter, and things in the States looked bad; hard talk in Washington and bad blood all over the country. I didn't like the way them South fellers talked. I was Dimicrat. Dad was, and I was. But I ain't never been one to crow and flop my wings when I was licked; it's the other rooster's place to do that, and it's his right, too.

"As I sensed it all up, it ranged itself in my head that the Dimicrats and the South put up a man or two men for President, and the Republicans and the North beat 'em, and their man was elected fair and square, and 'twarn't no fair play for the Dimicrats and the South to kick. 'Twas a fair fight and they was licked; and it riled me, too, to have sich talk 'bout the whole country, my country, being nothing but a lot of States, every one it's own boss, no captin, like a bunch of ranchers after Injuns, every one going it on his own hook.

"There warn't no sense in the idee. 'Twas the dangdest tomfoolery ever was, Bud. Then the Southern fellers said one of 'em could lick five Northern men, and the North wouldn't fight; and some feller said he was going to call the roll of his slaves on Bunker Hill, and I knew differnt.

"I was kinder on the fence like; born down in Southern Injianny; father and mother both come from North Caroliny; but perhaps because I was setting high on the fence I could see both sides clearer than them in either field could. I saw that the North they was stubborn and didn't say much, and I knew there was fight there; both sides were dead in earnist, and I felt bad.

"Yank and I didn't say much; course we talked 'bout other things, and each of us knew why we didn't talk. I was kinder Southern in my feelings, and I knew he was for the North straight. There was never no time before we didn't say everything we thought to each other. We worked together, and course we talked 'bout the work and things of no account, but I mean we never talked of the troubles, and both on us knew we were thinking 'bout them all the time. We both felt bad, but he was dead North and I was kinder South. When we got a paper, we would read it, and Yank would say, 'That was a danged smart thief, stole a man's watch from his pocket on Sansome Street, while he was a-looking at a fire.' And I would say, 'I never see such a cussed year for rain; been a-raining all the time in Californy, 'cording to the paper;' but never a word 'bout all the news we saw, that went clean to our toes as we read it. Somehow we was kinder gettin' apart, Yank an' me, who had been brothers, and I couldn't stand it. Yank was so kind of soft like to me in all ways, and that went to my heart, I kin tell ye.

"Grub was scarce with us; we had flour enuf, but meat was scarce. Yank wouldn't eat no bacon; said he was afeered of biles; I knew he only did it so there would be more for me. I couldn't stand it to see him going it on only bread, for we didn't have no coffee, nothing but flour and mighty little bacon. I wouldn't eat the bacon, and Yank got mad, said it seemed as if the devil was in me to try and drive him to eat bacon, and be covered from head to foot with biles. He'd be damned if any man was going to force hog down him when the idee made him sick, and cavorted and carried on so, I had to eat it. Ye couldn't do nothing with Yank. And one night we had only a couple of blankits each and 'twas cold. I was a-laying awake thinking of all the trouble I felt was a-coming, and how Yank and I seemed to be getting apart, shivering with the cold, too. I heered Yank coming still to my bunk, and he put a blankit on me softly, and I couldn't hold in no longer. 'What ye doing, Yank?' I said. 'I'm so thundering hot,' says he, 'I was going to throw off this blankit, and I thought ye might be cold, and I put it on ye; ye warn't born in Maine, and ye feel the cold.'

"I tried hard to make him take it back, and lied to him, and said I was warm.

"'How cussed contrary ye are getting, Zeb,' he said. 'What's the matter with ye? Ye ain't yerself any more; yer so dang peevish.'

"He wouldn't hear to nothing, and so the blankit stayed with me. If there was any hard end to the work he would have it, and if I said anything he was so short and cross, and so it went.

"One day he said to me something 'bout my working in the summer, and I said, 'We'll see 'bout that when the summer comes,' and Yank says, 'I may go East this summer. Haven't seen my folks for a long time.' He warn't thinking 'bout his folks, and I knew it.

"The winter went along, and every paper we see things were gittin' worse. All the talk of seceding made me mad.

"'Twas long in April, nigh the first of May, when a man come by. We was both of us at the mouth of the shaft, and the man said it was the story on the outside that the South had fired on some government forts down there, and that "Old Abe" had called for volunteers to go and fight. Yank questioned him quiet like 'bout it all, but the man didn't know more and went on.

"Both on us knew 'twas all true.

"We was a-setting on a timber we was a-going to let down the shaft. When the man was gone I see the fight was in Yank's eyes, and 'twas in my heart, too.

"Yank put his hand on my knee. 'Zeb,' said he, 'this means me. We've been pardners through thick and thin. I love ye, Zeb, but I must leave ye. Ye has yer idees, I have mine. I'm going to the States. Uncle Sam has called for his men and I'm a-going to his call. My grandfather fit in the Revolution and his father before him in the old French wars; my father was with Commodore Porter in the Essex, and when the Stars and Stripes are going to the fight it ain't in my blood to stay behind if the President calls for me to foller. I don't say nothing, Zeb, 'bout what's right or what's wrong, God knows. I only think I know. The fight is on; it's my President that calls me to go, and I am a-going. Ye are sort of Southern, Zeb, and ye don't see things as I see 'em; and, old man, it's hard to leave ye, but I'm a-going. I give ye all my interest in what we've got, and all good be with ye, Zeb.'

"I warn't never mad with Yank afore, but then I was, and I said, 'Yank, I'm going too. It's my country and my flag, and my President calls, and he don't call twice for me, if I am from Injianny nigh the river. Ye had it in yer mind, though ye didn't say it, that I was going to shirk this fight—me, Yank, me, who ye ought to know by this time. I've got my pride, if I am from Injianny, and I tell ye Injianny will be in it same as Maine. Damn it, Yank, this is my country, same as it's yours, and we'll go together, pardners, same as we've always been. Don't ye think I've got no feelings, Yank? I claim to be a man, and I'm ready to do a man's work. I see the work, and I'm going to do it. Ye've hurt me, Yank,' I said; 'ye've hurt me, me who ye have been pardner with so long. Did ye think I was going to be a woman when 'twas time to be a man? Shame on ye for it.'

"With that, Yank jumped up and swore and hugged me.

"'Why, Zeb,' he says, 'it's been on my mind all winter that ye were for the South and I've rasseled with the idee at night, and I thought, "Zeb's a man and he has his notions, and it ain't for one man to argy with another 'bout sich a thing, it is or it isn't; a man has a mind made up, he's going to do what he thinks is the squar thing to do, and it's no thing to talk," but I thought ye were for the South.'

"'The South be damned,' says I, 'and the North, too; I'm for the country, and the old flag.'

"Yank was like a boy, he was so glad, and he said:

"'Them Southern fellers say that one on 'em can lick five on us. Well, if one on 'em tackle us both and licks us, 'twill surprise me like hell;' and he laffed, and I did too, for I knew it would take a mighty good man to lick Yank single-handed, and with me on the outside to help, I didn't believe we'd ever find the man could do it. We was all so glad to be all friends agin same as before.

"Yank said, 'We'll quit this dang hole now,' and we did. We dropped the tools right there, and for all I know they're there now. We got up the hosses, we had one each, and two pack-hosses. There warn't no railroad then, and if there had been we hadn't no money, and we made it up we'd cross the plains to Iowy, and inlist in the first place we could. We had only a little grub, and we didn't know how we'd make it so far; we reckoned, then it was 'bout the first of May, we could make Iowy by August, but how was we to get grub?

"We talked all over and didn't see no way. At last, Yank, he says, 'Dang it, Zeb, we've got the call, and we ain't going to hang back 'cause we ain't got grub. We hain't no money to go by sea, and it's a long pull to the "Bay," anyway; we've got to go 'cross the plains. We'll go on what grub we've got, and take chances on getting more.' Next morning we packed up and started.

"It's an all-fired ride to the States. We was in a hurry to git there, and the time seemed longer than it was. We made it though; got to Iowy.

"We come into a little town on foot. We'd swapped off the outfit for grub on the way, from time to time; a hoss here and another one there, and one died, and our guns had to go, too. It was nigh September, and, as I said, we come into a little place in Iowy on foot, hungry and ragged and pretty well beat out. An old man was standing at the gate of one of them little white houses with a white fence round it, grass and sun-flowers and hollyhocks in the yard, and a trail through the grass to the door, straight as a gun-barrel.

"'Ye look like ye was used up,' said the old man. 'Yes,' said Yank, 'ye've hit the bull's eye, uncle. We've come a long way to go for soldiers, and we want to know where we can jine.'

"At that the old man made us come in, and drew a big bottle on us, and we must drink, and then we must eat, and we must stay with him over night, and his old woman—well, she was that kind we must eat this and that, and she wouldn't take no back talk from us. She told us how she had three boys in the army, and read us a letter that come that day from one.

"There was going to be a meeting that night, and speaking—a Union meeting, they called it—and there was a rigiment of men raising, and at the meeting volunteers could go up and sign, and the old man said there would be a fine lot of boys in it, and that the kernel was a man he knew, and he was going to be there, and he was a good man, but he thought he was too quiet like to be much of a fighter.

"So when we had washed up and had supper, we went with the old folks into the village. We was kind of 'shamed, for we looked like the devil; ragged we was, and our buckskin shirts pretty black, but we warn't dirty, for we were bound to sign with clean hands, anyway. As we went down the street there was a band a-playin' in front of a church, and into it we went with a lot of folks who looked at us like we was Injuns. Pretty soon ye couldn't get a card in edgewise, the house was that full. A parson prayed, and then some men spoke all about how the Union must be kept solid, and asking the young men to jine the company that was making up in the village, and every once in a while the band would play 'Yankee Doodle,' and 'The Star Spangled Banner,' and some young gals, putty as picturs, sang war songs, and it all made the blood come and go, I tell ye, Bud.

"Then a little man got up and said how he was to be the kernel of the rigiment; and while he warn't much of a talker, his heart was in the fight and he meant to be as good a soldier as it was in him to be. I took to the feller right off. I see he was a man, if he was small; and Yank he chucked me and says, 'He's our man, Zeb.'

"Yank knew a man when he saw one, and he sized the little feller up then, and I tell ye he sized him up right, too. But everybody was kind of sneering at the man, and a feller behind says in a low voice, 'That little cuss is no good. Looks like he'd run better than he'd fight.'

"'If that's your idee, it ain't mine,' Yank said to him.

"Then they put a big paper on a little table that was under the pulpit, and the kernel says, 'Who's the first man to put his name down for his country?'

"'I am,' says Yank, 'and my pardner, Zeb, he's with me,' and up he goes with me and down we put our names on the papers.

"'Where are ye from?' says the kernel.

"'We've come from Nevady,' says Yank.

"'How'd ye get here?' says the kernel.

"'We heer'd the call and we saddled up and come,' says Yank.

"'What,' says the kernel, 'ye rode on hossback two thousand miles, to inlist?'

"'Yes,' says Yank. 'We rode and we hoofed it. We know we're strangers, but ye'll find we've come for business. No better man ever stood than Zeb, here, my pardner, and I'll try and keep up with him.'

"I was 'shamed to hear Yank say so 'bout me, and I said, 'Yank's a better man nor me. Why, Yank—there ain't no more sandier man in all the world than him. We'll do our duty, both on us, to the country and to the flag. Ye don't know us, but try us.'

"'Then,' says the kernel, 'here are two men that

heer'd the call in the desert, and they've come two thousand miles to inlist. Come, boys, show them that there are men in Iowy, too.'

"That's all he said, but the way he said it beat all the speeches that was made, and the young men rose up all over the church, and come up and put their names down, and there was nigh to sixty come up, but the kernel says, 'That ain't enough. I won't leave here this night till the roll has a hundred names on it.'

"Then up gits the parson, and a gritty, young-looking fellow he was, and he says, 'There's a time for men to preach and there comes a time for men to fight. The call of the country, that two thousand miles away, beyond the plains and the mountains these men heer'd, has been sounding in my heart for months, and to-night I answer, "Yes, Father Abraham, I'm a-coming,"' and up he goes and signs the roll.

"I thought the church would bust with the cheering, and men went up two or three at a time and signed, and the men cheered, and women were a-crying, and in ten minutes the roll was full and more—a hundred and seven names.

"It warn't many days afore the rigiment was a full thousand men strong. The parson was made captin of the company we was in, and the kernel he says to Yank, 'What can I do for you, Yank?' and Yank says, 'Kernel, I wants to carry the flag and I want Zeb with me, and Zeb and I'll carry her where she's got to go, and we'll stay with her.' So the kernel he made Yank color-sargeant and puts me in the color-guard so as to be near him.

"I always thought the Stars and Stripes made a

fine show. I knew it was my country's flag and my flag, but bless ye, Bud, I didn't know nothing afore 'bout what that flag is, and what it means, and how a man gets to love it and be proud to his death of it; how it comes to mean everything ; how it stands for everything a man loves; how it is a man's pride and his glory. His father and his grandfather and so back had it for their flag; all on 'em lived under it, some on 'em fought under it, some on 'em died under it.

"When ye were a small boy it meant trainings and fairs, and Fourth of July, and everything that was out of the common run. There never was no jollification that ye didn't see it a-waving overhead; round the fire at night yer father told ye 'bout the last war, and ye could see in yer little cub mind the flag a-flyin', and hear the drums and fifes a-playin', as yer father, long with all the rest, charged the Britishers at Lundy's Lane or held the cotton bales agin 'em at New Orleans; or yer old grandfather made the tears come in yer little eyes as he told how, when he was a boy, at Valley Forge, in cold and starvation, his frozen feet and hungry belly was warm and full when day come, and he could see the flag a-waving; and yer little heart got big as he told the story how at Yorktown the men who come to fight us marched prisoners before the Stars and Stripes, saluting of 'em. Ye began to be a man then, and the flag come to mean something.

"But ye don't know nothing 'bout it, Bud, till ye foller it; ye gits to love it. It ain't a pretty piece of cloth, the totem of yer tribe, it's all there is of everything; it's country, it's memry, it's hope. All that's good and squar in ye comes to love it. Yer wet and tired and hungry a-follering of it; ye lose yer blood and yer life for it and it's all a pleasure.

"It's a-waving in the air so much cloth at so much a yard; it lies in yer heart, all the gold and the silver in the mountains; all the ships on the sea; all the farms, and the towns; and all the sweat and blood of them that's dead and gone, the joy and pride of them alive, the hope and cheer of them to come.

"Well, Yank, he carried the flag, and I was with him, with a few as fit men as ye ever see to guard it.

"Our company was 'C' Company, and the colors is always nigh 'C' Company, so all our boys as we were in line was 'long side.

"The parson who we made captin was a fine, straight young man. He was like an egg, the white all mild and pious and good, and the yelk all fight. Dang'd if I hain't thought a heap of parsons since I knew him. He'd preach like Billy be damn'd and fight like hell the same day; he was an all 'round man, I tell ye, but all through he stuck to his trade, as I likes to see a man do; never no swearing. I never could see how he did it; it's such a real comfort to cuss sometimes and it comes so nateral to a man.

"Well, we was sent down into Kentucky and into Tennessee; we marched a many miles and had many tight fights, and Yank was hit a couple of times, and I, too, light like, nothing to count. We was at Pittsburgh Landing and all them fights, and we was proud of the fellows we was with. The kernel he was a fighter from way back, though he was so small and quiet, and the captin—the parson—there warn't no nervier man, and all the boys stood right into the collar. They all got to know Yank, and nobody warn't afeer'd 'bout the flag being carried by a man.

"Yank was one of them men who put his whole body, head, belly, and boots into anything he did; a-prospecting, a-hunting, a-playin' a game, going to preachings, 'twas all the same, and he was all in that war. He didn't talk nothing else, he didn't think nothing else.

"What come hard to me was to be ordered here and there, and be under somebody all the time, but that didn't faze Yank a bit.

"'Zeb,' he used to say, 'ye must get the right savvy of this business. A ship has a captin and she has mates, and in some ships some on 'em are poor men. Ye know yer a better man nor them, but ye've got to obey orders; ye ain't sailin' the ship, yer just doing what yer told to do, that's yer business. It's the same here; I do my business, and ye do yours, and it don't consarn ye, nor I, nothing else.'

"All his idee was the flag, and we all see it, and 'twas our idee too.

"So it went along, marching and fighting, big fights and little ones, long marches and short ones, till it come we were under General Thomas at Chattanoogy. There was a sizable hill and the Johnnies was on the hill. In the morning when we come up to the kernel's tent to get the colors, the kernel himself come out and give the flag to Yank, and he says, 'It's going to be a hot day, and please God we'll have the colors top o' the hill 'fore night.'

"'If there's a show, the flag will be there all right, Kernel; Zeb, he'll carry it there, if I don't,' says Yank.

"'We mayn't either of us git there, but the rigimint will, Yank,' says the kernel; 'I feel it somehow.'

"'I hain't no other idee,' says Yank.

"I never was so afore. I looked at Yank, and he looked kind o' strange, and I felt something was a-coming. We had it all put up from the first day Yank carried the flag. Says he to me: 'When I drop, Zeb, you take the flag; if ye leave me a-dyin' the flag must go on. If ye've got anything to say, "Good-by" or "God bless ye," say it now; for if I drop, the flag must go, mind that, Zeb. I'd die a-cussing ye if ye stopped a second for me. Yer my pardner—dang it, Zeb, yer my brother—and man to man I want ye to say after me these words: "When ye, Yank, drops and can't go on or hold up the flag, I'll take it and go on. If I see yer dying I won't stop to say a word or nothing. I'll take the flag and leave ye where ye lie. I'll carry it and guard it, and die with it if so be I must. So help me God Almighty!" Hold up yer right hand,' he says, 'and say them very words after me.'

"'Oh, Yank,' I said, 'I couldn't leave ye so, I couldn't. I, yer long pardner.'

"'What,' says Yank, and them gray eyes of his looked like a cougar's in the dark, and his voice was so hard and changed; 'ye'd go agin me when I was a-dyin'? Ye'd refuse to give me comfort at such a time? Ye'd have me go afore God a-cussin' ye? Ye'd leave the flag, my flag, to any one else, or a-laying on the ground where I dropped it, while ye played the baby with me? Ain't there any man in ye, Zeb? Ain't there any friend in ye, Zeb? Ain't there any pride in ye for me? When I asked for to carry this flag, 'twas because I thought I had a man that would take it when my hands couldn't hold it no longer; that, if so be I was a-dyin', my eyes would see him going on with it. Didn't we go into this fight 'cause we felt it was a duty and we must? The man that's got the flag he's got his duty to do to his country; the flag has got to be carried, and the man who carries it can't stop to palaver over nobody's carkiss.'

"'Oh, Yank,' I said, 'I sees my duty, and I'll do it, but 'twould come rough the way ye put it.'

"'Yer a man,' Yank said, 'and yer a woman, but I know ye; say them words.' And I held up my right hand and said the words after him.

"When we first got into fights, I was afeered for Yank, but we had been in a many of 'em, and only two shots had hit him, and only one, me, and all on 'em no 'count, much more nor scratches, and somehow my fear 'bout him had got over; but that morning I felt something was a-coming.

"We didn't have much to do all morning, drawn up in a line to go in, and waiting orders. The battle had been going on for a couple of hours; we could see some of it and hear more, for the firing was heavy to the right of us, and the cannons was a-roaring.

"We was standing there and lying on the ground, Yank and me a-smoking. The kernel had rode the line talking to the captins, and he come where we was.

"'Yank,' he says, 'and ye too, Zeb, I've mentioned ye both in reports, but I never did tell ye what I couldn't say then, and what I have wanted to say to ye both for a long time. Ye did more to raise this rigiment than I did, and all along ye have been good men, and I have to thank ye both. It isn't my fault, Yank, that yer not a commissioned officer,' and 'twas so; for twice he had Yank to be an officer, but Yank wouldn't have it; his idee was all to carry the flag. We was proud to hear the kernel say that, for he warn't no man to talk.

"We was a-smoking when a young officer come a-riding up and says something to the kernel, and the order come sharp to the rigiment, putting us into column, and we marched up over a rise of ground and past some woods where we could see the hill, 'Missionary Ridge' was the name of it. Yank took the pipe from his mouth, a short clay pipe it was, and give it to me. 'Keep that, Zeb,' he said, and I put it in my pocket. It's in my bag now,'' the old man said. "I've kept it. We could see the hill all spotted here and there with rigimints and brigades, some high up and some low down, and the smoke coming from their guns on both sides. The trees hid what was going on in places, and then there would be clearings where we could see putty good.

"The Johnnies had two or three lines of earthworks, and the fighting was a-going on where the lower line was mostly, but in one place we could see the lower line was carried, and our boys was up agin the next one.

"The other rigimints of our brigade had come up, and we was put in line agin, and right in front of us, and perhaps a half a mile away, the hill began to rise up sharp, and along the steep side we could see two lines of dirt where the rifle-pits was, and behind 'em we could see the tops of the baynits and the flagstaffs of the men behind, when the sun came through the clouds to shine on 'em. Everywhere else, 'cept opposite where we was, we could see either the men or the smoke they made, but there warn't no smoke or show of fight in front of us. It was our place.

"Well, as I said, the line was formed, and pretty soon the orders come to go ahead, and we marched toward the hill. The cannons was a-firing, but they didn't do much harm; ye can't catch the range on a cannon like ye can on a rifle.

"We come up to the front of the hill in good shape, and then they halted us a bit to take breath and to straighten the line.

"The hill above us was steep, and the rifle-pits we could see here and there the lines of between the trees, seemed right over us; and when we could see them at all, there was the Johnnies back of 'em, with their gun-barrels slanting down at us, and 'specially where we was a-going there was a clear strip of ground clean up to the pits; not a tree, hardly a bush a rabbit could get behind. I never see no sich place for men to go agin. Yank, he says to me, 'Zeb, mind what ye swore to, and if I don't get the flag to the top ye will.' 'I'll keep my word, Yank,' says I, 'but we'll get there together, or it's as like I'll drop as will ye.'

"I hadn't much idee we'd either of us get there, it was such a dang tough place.

"The kernel he see how it was, and tried how he could manage it to get us to each side of the clear strip, but there warn't room. The other rigiments were up agin ours on either end of our line, and there warn't no time; for while he was a-studying on it come the order to forward up the hill.

"The kernel took his place just behind the color-guard, and most of 'C' Company and the next was in the clear strip, and we with the colors 'bout in the middle of it.

"In the picturs ye see of battles, Bud, ye'll always see the gineral or the kernel a-riding on ahead and a-waving of his sword and a-calling to the men to come on. The fellers who made them picturs don't know nothing. The officers' place is behind the men, and it's right and proper it's so. When it gets hot and mixed a bit, the officers is sometimes ahead; but when the thing goes on right, the men are in front and every officer has his place behind.

"We'd gone up the hill till we was, say, 'bout three hundred yards from the Johnnies behind the pits; it was hard climbing, enough to blow us a little, and the drums and fifes stopped playing, and ye only heer'd the officers a-saying, 'Close up, close up,' and trying to keep the line straight.

"We was expecting hell would pop every second, but it didn't. As we was 'bout three hundred yards or so from 'em, as I say, we heer'd the officers a-calling to the Johnnies, and up they got and let us have it, but though it knocked many a feller, it warn't so bad, we was so under 'em like. Then comes the order to 'Charge,' and at the hill we went, the shots coming down on us like hail stones and the men a-falling fast. I see Yank drop his arm like, and I said, 'yer hit.'

"''Tain't nothing,' he says, 'didn't hit no bone.' Just then come the order from the kernel to 'Fire,' and we picked 'em off the top of the rifle-pits like they was crows on a fence. Then it was 'Load' again. 'Hold yer fire,' he says to our company; and the next, 'Let no man fire till he gets the order;' but the other companies was a-putting in the lead fast as they could.

"We'd got up to, say, sixty or seventy yards, perhaps the half on us was left, and there was some rocks in a line; 'twas like an old fence, and the ground kind of sheltered us a little. We was halted there and dropped to what cover we could find. The breath was pretty well out of us and we was a-ketching of it again.

"Yank was a-bleeding and I put a handkerchief round his arm. I could see the ground behind us spotted with men down and dead. The kernel's horse was dead, and he a-walking and a-resting nigh us behind a rock. He crawled out a bit, and he says, 'See yer all loaded and we'll go over the pits next trip. Yank,' he says, 'when we charge, do ye go over the pits and we'll all be with ye.'

"I could see the ends of the rigiment was close on to the pits on both sides of us, but there was nothing but grass between us and the Johnnies, and right straight up it was. We'd a-rested two or three minutes or so, the bullets a-cracking agin the rocks and picking a man now and then who couldn't cover. 'Zeb,' says Yank, to me, 'there's a rock a little to the left on us nigh the pits, and there the earth ain't thrown so high; I'll make for that and ye all rush over with me.'

"There was only three of the color-guard left, but 'twas all the same. Nigh us was Jim Jackson and Dan Pinder and a lot of other sandy men. I passed the word to 'em and the others, and the captin—he'd wormed 'long 'till he was with us—he passed the word to the company to head for that pint in the rifle-pits.

Then come the kernel's voice sharp and loud, and we stood up in front of the rock and got into line a-cheering. Up rose the Johnnies for a volley at us, and we pulled trigger at the kernel's 'Fire.'

"Lord, how we downed 'em! 'Forward, double quick, charge!' cried the kernel, and we went for 'em on the run, but they kept a-giving it to us quick and hot. Jackson dropped, and Pinder's brains spurted in my face, but we made the rock and got on to the top of the earthwork. Then the Johnnies come hand to hand with us. The captin and the kernel and may be a dozen more was there, but we couldn't budge the solid line of men, and we was a-dropping fast. There warn't no time to load—'twas hand to hand. The captin and the kernel's sword was everywhere; my baynit I broke in a man's breast. The kernel fell, shot in the head. Yank planted the colors behind him in the soft ground, and caught up Billy Lee's gun when he was run through, and he and me we cleared the spot round us with our muskits. We swung 'em like they was clubs. Yank was a stout man and I was fair, and many a time the heads would crack when we brought the gun-barrels down on 'em.' 'Twarn't a minute, but I see the captin run through, and Yank and I was alone.

"'Give 'em hell, Zeb!' he cried, and I never see no man like him then. His eyes was a-blazing, the flag behind him, and his back agin the staff. He got a shot in the leg, and he had to drop on his knees. I caught it in the neck and another in my shoulder, and a baynit pricked me in the side, but still we kept 'em off.

"A big feller had been a-working closer to us, a

long-haired cuss, and he whips out a six-shooter and p'ints it at Yank. There was a man on me, but I caught him with the heel of the gun, and I brought the barrel down on the long-haired feller and smashed his head in, but 'twas too late, Bud, 'twas too late; his gun went off and took Yank in the head.

"'The flag, Zeb,' he said, and he was gone. I warn't no man, then, I was a devil. I knew our fellers begun a-getting up to me. I can't 'member no more, but they said I caught up the flag and jumped agin the Johnnies like a cougar from a tree. Where we was—though 'twarn't no time, I 'spose, we was on the top—was the only place in the line that warn't carried, and when our boys had got both sides they closed down on the place, and so just as I took the flag, they come in like bees and drove the crowd agin us a-surging up the hill. But I was after 'em, and all was, and up we went agin the next line, and I over it and the boys a-follerin'; all I knew was, I was a carryin' of the flag. I got on top with the flag, Yank's flag, and then I dropped.

"'Twas a great battle, and there was lots like me, a-wounded, and I come to in a big hospitil tent. I put out my hand a-feeling for Yank—we always slept under the same blankits. 'Yank,' I called, and the doctor of my rigiment he was nigh, and he sot down on the bed, and, 'Zeb,' he says, 'Yank's gone out.'

"Then it all come to me, and I says, 'Out of the world; he's gone to heaven.' And I was that weak I cried like a baby; but he give me some stuff and I dozed off. I come to myself right in a day or so more, and I knew I'd have to go it alone. Yank was gone. I didn't care to live, first off, and then the idee come to me how I was kinder to carry out Yank's notions, and I spruced up. 'Yes, Yank,' I said, 'I'll see the thing through, and I won't be easy till the flag that was yer pride has it's own agin.'

"There was lots of the boys 'round me. The captin was two or three beds away, a-gitting on right smart, and he told me how it all was.

"The major come in and he said, as how the rigiment was cut up, we was a-going into camp till we got some more boys down from Iowy to take the places of them that was killed. They was all kind to me, and one day the gineral he come in and he come down the line of beds.

"'Where's Zeb?' he says, and comes up to me so sociable, and he talked like I was an officer, and calls me 'looytennant.' 'I'm only a corporal, Gineral,' I says. 'Yer a looytennant,' he says. 'I sent in yer name when I see ye top of the ridge with the flag.' The tears come in my eyes.

"'Gineral,' I says, 'it's kind of yer, and I feel it, I do, but I want to carry the flag;' and I told him how Yank and me was old pardners, and how his idee was all to carry the flag, and how he kinder left it to me to carry when he was gone, and that I wanted to carry it, if he'd let me, and he swore, and says: 'Zeb, ye shall. No man shall ever carry that flag so long as you kin, but you;' and he took my hand and he says, 'Such men as you and yer pardner make a country great.' Yes, he said that. 'Lord,' says I, 'Gineral, I didn't do nothing. After Yank was gone I was wild, and I didn't know nothing.'

"'Well,' he says, 'it's wild men like you who make us ginirals lots of glory we don't desarve;' and he took my hand, and he come agin two or three times, and we was mighty friendly. Dang'd if he didn't send me grub and cigars till ye couldn't rest.

"After a while I was all right, and went back to the rigiment, and they give me the flag to carry. Lord, how I loved it! 'Twas all torn with bullits and the staff was nicked here and there, and I remembred one of them nicks well, but the cuss that made it, I see the kernel—'twas the last thing he did afore he was killed—cut him down with his sword through the skull.

"I carried the flag all the war. I was hit agin, but not so bad as to have to drop it. I carried it with Sherman on the March to the Sea, and I carried it before the President at the Great Review in Washington; and when I left it, I cut a piece from it—I asked the giniral, and he said I might—that's in the buckskin sack I've got. How I hated to leave it, 'count of Yank! But Lord, 'twarn't that identical piece of cloth he was stuck on, 'twas all on 'em; that was Yank's idee."

CHAPTER IX

The great storm which had closed the old and opened the new year had been succeeded by clear and beautiful weather, and all through January and into February no snow fell, and so vigorously had work been carried on, that the cut was now nearly under the shaft. The pans of gravel that were daily, and of late several times a day, tried, began to show even more gold than before. One morning, Zeb, who was at work in the face of the cut, struck his pick on something which he thought he recognized, and quickly scooping out with his shovel the dirt his pick loosened, he made a little hole. Bud, who was wheeling as he broke down the gravel, had just come up with the empty wheelbarrow.

"Bed-rock, Bud, bed-rock," cried the old man, as between his fingers and thumb he felt of a gray soft substance on the end of his shovel; "and look at it, see the gold in it. That's it, Bud. We've made the riffle at last."

Bud saw the gray matter sprinkled with little grains of gold, and put the shovel on the ground, with his finger poking its contents. "Here's big gold, Zeb," as a piece the size of a ten-cent piece struck his eye, and turning with it in his hand, he saw Zeb sitting on the wheelbarrow, with his head in his hands, very still. "Zeb, old man," he said, catching at him, "we have it; we have it."

"Yes, Bud," said Zeb, "we have it, God be thanked! It's struck me all of a heap. I've been in Injianny, Bud. Never do ye doubt them signs agin; it's awful to do it. I see that bear and them cubs where I see that bed-rock. Let this be a lesson to ye, Bud. 'God works in a mysterious way his wonders to perform.' That is good Bible, and that's what Yank would say if he was here. I'm that thankful I'd give a year of my life if I could think what to say. Ye don't know what the gold means to me, Bud. Ye can't know how from my toes up I thank God; and dang ornery cuss that I am, I can't think of no fit words but 'Thank ye, thank ye, God Almighty.' All them words is in my heart that my tongue can't speak. Oh, Lord, if Yank was here!" and throwing himself on his knees, "Thank ye, thank ye," he cried, with face uplifted, and with such simple fervor that, rude as was the prayers wrung from lips so unused to supplication or to acknowledgment of benefits, it seemed to Bud to cleave its way through air into infinite space to the ears of the Infinite Ruler of all.

They took a pan from the bed-rock, and what a pan of dirt that was! The grains, big and little, with occasional pieces as large as a pea, lay thick when the dirt was all gone. "There's ten dollars in that—no, there's seven or eight," said Zeb; and they panned another pan which was not so good, but had, as they estimated, three dollars in it, and another that had less than that, and another that was nearly as good, and others, until Zeb said:

"It is there, and it won't get away from us. We'll put up sluice-boxes, and when the days are warm we'll get a little water from the spring and we'll make a rocker, and between using the water when the snow is melting, and the rocker when we hain't much water, we'll be taking gold out every day, and in six week's time we'll have all the water we can handle, and we'll sluice out a fortune. We've got it rich, Bud. Even if it's only a pocket, there's big money in it. We've got to dig that ditch, and as it gets warm—sometimes does along now—we'll have our water. We can't do no more good here; let's go right to work on that ditch."

Five feet of snow covered the ground, and it was well they had, before it came, surveyed the line of the ditch, for, digging in the snow, they could find the little stakes they had driven in the ground to mark its course. In ten days the ditch was finished and ready for the first melting of the snow.

During this time, as they sat at evening about the fire, Zeb's happiness was overflowing. "Do ye know, Bud," he said one night, "I've been a-thinking this money has got to go somewhere, and life's onsartin; but, live or die, my sheer of this money has got to go somewhere, and I suppose ye've something you want to do with yours. What I've got to say is this: If anything happens to me, I want you to send my sheer of the dust we git to Jim Peasley, Poseytown, Injianny, and write a letter to him how it was I pegged out, if so be I do. I'll write a letter and give ye, and ye kin put it in the letter ye write. I know I kin trust ye, if anything happens, to do the right thing."

"That you can, Zeb."

"Well, write it down; ye've got pen and ink. Jim Peasley, Poseytown, Injianny. See he gits the dust, or the money it brings, and don't ye go to no bank to do it, but Wells, Fargo, Bud. And now 'bout your sheer."

"Well, Zeb, I haven't thought about it. I hardly know."

"See here, Bud, this thing must be done ship-shape."

"I don't know, and I don't care much;" and thinking a minute, "you can send mine to a name I'll write, and I'll write a letter too, that you can send."

"Give me your hand on it, then. I couldn't be quiet in my grave, if I ever have one, if anything should happen to the money," the old man said.

They took each other's hand on it, and Bud, getting the pen and ink and paper, wrote a short letter, and sealed it in an envelope, which he directed. "Here's mine," he said; "send to the address on the letter, and the letter with it."

Zeb awkwardly took the pen, and laboriously devoted a full hour to covering two sides of a sheet of paper, and, putting it in an envelope, handed the pen to Bud. "Write ye," he said, "Jim Peasley, Poseytown, Injianny," which Budd did, and sealed the envelope. The two letters were carefully put away on the little shelves near their bunk. "Now I feel better," said Zeb. "I've had this on my mind ever sence we struck the bed-rock. Bud," he said, "'tain't no business of mine, but 'pears like ye don't feel no better than ye did afore we struck it. Dang'd if ye've been as peart as ye was; seems like ye don't care nothing 'bout it."

"Well, Zeb, I don't care much, that's true. I do care, for you are pleased; but for myself, it don't matter. Money, or no money, it's all the same."

The old man's kind, clear eyes looked at his young companion searchingly, and he started to speak, but checked himself, and sat in silence for some time. At last he said: "There's no man I've taken to sence Yank died like I has to ye, Bud. Ye've made a friend of me; ye hain't put on no airs with me. I'm ignorant, and I'm old-fashioned. I've been so long in the mountains that dang'd if I know anything else. Ye've come of good folks, and yer eddicated. All yer life, till ye come with me, ye've had life go easy with ye. Ye've never been in rough places, nor had to do with rough folks. Yer a gentleman, and ye've lived the life of them in cities, and it ain't that I put myself to larn ye anything; but, Bud, I love ye like ye was my own son. Yes, my boy, I do; and there's a kind of larning that comes with years and ain't taught in schools, nor a young man don't get it from the company he keeps, if it is high company.

"Bud, yer wrong, yer wrong. Whatever has happened to ye, I don't want to know it; I don't ask to know it; but I can see yer wrong in the way ye take it. What years larns a man to do is to remember to forgit. Yer remembering everything; ye ain't forgitting anything. Now we'll suppose," and he looked keenly at him as he spoke, " ye had some trouble, and ye waited till the feller drew on ye, and then ye nailed him; now, what ye want to remember is that if he had got a second shot at ye he'd 'a' killed ye, and what ye want to forgit is that he was a man; he was a cougar when he come for ye." And, with his eyes still fixed on him, "We'll suppose ye got in love—men mostly do some time—and the girl wouldn't have ye; then ye want to remember that lots of men has done the same thing afore, and what ye want to forgit is that she's the only woman in the world."

Feeling that he had illustrated his meaning by taking as examples all the possible causes that could have brought worry to his friend, Zeb added, "If I had not had this larning come to me, I'd be a miserable cuss, for I've been in both them places myself."

Bud was walking the floor of the little cabin. "Zeb," he said, "it's worse than that. Since I've gotten to know you, to realize what kind of a man you are, it has been on my lips to tell you something; but you are so true, you are so honest, Zeb. I ought to have told you before, but I could not do it, Zeb. They say I'm a thief; but here before God—I'm looking into your eyes, Zeb—it is a lie, a damnable lie. Yes, Zeb, they said I was a thief;" and sobs came from the young fellow as he walked the floor.

"Ye did right, Bud, ye did right. I'd killed him afore the words were out of his mouth. No man could do anything but that."

"I didn't kill any one, Zeb; I didn't touch him."

"Didn't kill him? Didn't touch him?" Zeb repeated in amazement. "Ye didn't have yer gun, and he got away?"

"No, Zeb, I did not touch him. You don't understand it. I love this man's niece. He has been a father to her, and I was in his employ; something was missed, and he said I stole it. It seemed as if it must have been me; everything pointed to me; everybody believes it. There is no proof to convict me before the law, but the judgment of man has made me a thief.

It's horrible; and she, the girl I love, she will believe it. Oh, God, it almost drives me wild! I don't think of it. I try to forget it, but it will come up. When I met you, Zeb, I was just from New York. I said to myself, 'There is no hope for me here.' I could not fight the charge, for none was publicly made. I could not remain there. I felt, for the sake of the one I loved, I must get out of her way, and so I left, with no idea where I was going, with no care where I went, hoping everybody would forget me. I bought a ticket to San Francisco. There was something in the air, or change of scene, that put vigor in me. As I rode along I said to myself, 'I will begin in a new country a new life. I will put the old one behind me. I will never go back to friends who have been so unjust, to associates so cruel.'

"The clear air, the bright skies, the wildness of the country calmed me. I met a man on the train, and we fell into conversation. He was going to Helena, in Montana, and because he did not know me, because he could not look on me with the suspicious eyes of those I had left behind, because he talked of the new country, he interested me, common, vulgar, scheming creature though he was; and as he was going, he told me to ride from Helena to some mines he had—they were in such a wild country. I was interested, and I thought to myself, 'I wish I could go into some place so wild that I could see no one,' and I asked him if I could go with him. He seemed pleased to have me, and so I went to Helena with him. There I bought the outfit that I have, for he told me what to get, and I paid for mine and for his, for it seemed he had no money. He would repay me at his mines. I did not care whether he ever paid me or not. I had my money all in large bills, and he could see it when I took it out.

"The day before we left Helena, I deposited in a bank twelve hundred dollars. He did not know of it —not that I cared—but it happened he was not with me, and I did not speak of it. I had about three hundred dollars more left, and I took it with me. We rode off and we camped, and all was new to me; everything interested me—the packing, the cooking, the free, independent air of it all. We had been riding several days, and I began to know this man, and I began to hate him as I did; he was so selfish and so mean and so low in his ideas. I was bored with him. I was anxious to get to our destination so that I might leave him. I had now a little knowledge of how to travel in a wild country, and I wished to be by myself, to go by myself, anywhere, it did not matter where. The next day we would reach his place, and the next day, and so on. One morning I awoke, and he and everything that belonged to him was gone. I went to my coat, which I had thrown on my saddle, and, as I expected, my pocket-book was gone. I cared so little, I was so glad he had gone, I was so pleased to get rid of him, I did not even regret the loss of my money. I was happy; I knew, whichever way I went, that in time I would meet some one, or cross some road; and if it would be a month before I did, it mattered not. My trouble was with my pack-horse and his pack, but I got along after a fashion. The third day, I met you, Zeb, and I was tired of being alone. There was something about you that I liked, and I asked to go with you. That's all my miserable story. Save one man, to whom I wrote the letter, and perhaps the woman I love, everybody believes me a thief. Perhaps, I say. Good God! I don't know, but she can't believe it; she can't believe it, Zeb. Tell me you don't believe this lie, Zeb; tell me that."

During this recital, Zeb's amazement had gradually given place to sympathy.

"I wouldn't have believed it of ye, Bud," he said. "I suppose city ways is differnt, and I allow for him being an uncle of the girl's, and all that, and ye young, too. I'll bet my life yer no thief," he said, taking the young man's hand; "but yer a fool, Bud, that's what ye are. I'm sorry for yer trouble; I'd give anything to help ye. Ye've been wrong 'bout it all. Ye've run away when ye ought to have staid right there and fought it out. Ye've given everybody a right to think ye did that thing. I can't see it no other way. I never see anything so misfortnit as the man being her uncle and a sort of father to her. Yes, perhaps ye couldn't kill him. I don't know; it's a hard question 'bout that.

"We'll take a trip this next summer, Bud, you and me, and we'll go to New York, and we'll camp right there till this thing's made straight. Now, don't ye have it on yer mind, boy; thar's nothing can be done now, and it's foolish to worry and wind yer hoss afore ye've got to use him.

"There's nobody here but thinks ye're a squar man; nobody here but loves ye. Dang it, Bud, ye've got like a son to me."

After having told his story, Bud felt a sense of relief. The sympathy and confidence of his companion in him were so grateful. It touched him to see how, in a thousand ways, Zeb tried to cheer him. He never spoke of it, but his efforts were made with so much delicacy, and were so unremitting, he could not fail to feel them.

CHAPTER X

As they had a chance, Zeb, and Bud acting under his instructions, made a rocker, something like a cradle, the bottom, set on an angle, resting on rounding pieces. One would bring the gravel, and the other would dip up and pour in the water and agitate the rocker. Often they would take out in a few hours what Zeb would estimate at fifty or sixty dollars; and there coming a little soft weather, they ran a little water through the sluice-boxes, and shovelling in the gravel as fast as the slight head of water would allow, they cleared up from the riffles in the bottom about ninety ounces of gold-dust. Their little store had augmented till now Zeb roughly calculated they had one hundred and thirty ounces of gold. This was put in a buckskin sack of the old man's making, and had such decided weight, it was a pleasure to lift it.

Sundays they took long walks on the snowshoes, Bud getting very expert in their use; they even extended their walks so that one day they made twenty-five miles. The probability of their "diggins," for so Zeb dignified them, demanding more water than they could conveniently reach near by, and which should furnish a supply all season, led Zeb to explore a big creek which, some distance above them, put into the river.

They walked up this creek, and calculated that, by

bringing in a ditch eight or nine miles long, ample water could be brought on their claim at a sufficient height above it to give a fall of two hundred feet or more for the pipes, Zeb explaining the manner of working hydraulic mines in a large way, as they went along. From where they had stopped to look at a place in the stream where Zeb thought would be an advantageous place to begin the contemplated ditch there ran by gradual descent a long, smooth mountain side.

"I would like to go up there, Zeb, and look off of the divide," said Bud. "It's a clear day; we could see a long distance."

"That ain't a bad idee. I'd like to kinder get the lay of the country myself," said the old man; "so go ahead."

They found it a long, hard climb, and three hours of active work elapsed before they stood on the summit; but the grand view before them well repaid the effort. A great white solitude, broken by patches of timber. Over this wintry waste the eye roamed in search of something that might indicate human presence, but there was nothing; unbroken solitude, nature at her wildest, and over her, winter's white blanket; not a cloud in the sky. The eye roamed for scores of miles over as unbroken a wilderness as our great land contains. Away at the north the brown, darker color showed the plains the hills had lapsed into; but west and east and south only broken mountain country with great peaks of dazzling whiteness rising high above the green spots of timber on their sides; great clefts, of which they could not see the bottom, showed where the Salmon and its tributaries made way. Off at the east and south sharply ran the jagged ridge of the Sawtooth Range, and the White Mountains, cold and still, like great domes of rounded marble, limited vision in their direction. The Weisers, Esty's Peak, and others afar off, the bright sun brought clearly out, while the innumerable smaller hills crowded around these giants, sitting at their feet with their green mantles of fir and pine drawn round them. Not a breath of air stirred; the stillness that can be felt, the quiet of a great loneliness, was over all.

"Where is there any one besides ourselves, Zeb?" at last Bud said. "One would think we were alone in the world."

"Let me see. Placerville must be about there," pointing to the south. "I reckon that's the nearest settlement; mebbe it's a hundred and twenty or thirty miles. Yes," continued Zeb, "it lies about that way. There's Bernard Mountain, and that's Scott's Peak, and it lies on beyond, across the Payette, about fifty miles or so farther."

"And is there no one nearer than that?"

"There's placer mines somewhere between here and Placerville, but it ain't likely there's any one there in winter; and there may be trappers somewhere round, but it ain't likely; this ain't no great fur country 'round here, no way."

The sun, now some distance past the zenith, began to cast shadows here and there, and gave a still colder aspect to the scene, for where they fell the snowy surface was steel gray.

"We'll have a great run down," said Zeb, "and we'd better be going, for it's quite a pull to camp."

They started down the mountain, and had a most

exhilarating run for three miles or more, doing it in ten minutes; and so quickly had Bud acquired the knack of riding the shoes, that he allowed them to take a pace Zeb did not keep up with, and arrived at the cabin after a good twenty-five mile round, little exhausted by the exertion of the day.

Day after day went by, and as the temperature allowed the water to run, they added to their stock of gold-dust. Another thaw gave so much of it that they could again shovel the gravel into the boxes, and so more dust went into the buckskin sacks, for there were now two of them. Bud became quite familiar with the work, and, as Zeb said, "took to it like an old timer."

In the running off of the gravel, a large boulder in it came to light, and as it was in the channel or line where was the richest ground, the miners had worked the gravel away from beneath it, and to keep it from falling on the bed-rock and being in their way, they had propped it up, holding it in place by an upright timber. The soft weather caused the water from the melting snow above to trickle down the side of the excavation from which this rock hung out, partly imbedded in the gravel and partly overhanging the bed-rock on which was set the timber supporting it.

It had been a soft night, and when work was begun in the morning, here and there the sides of the cut had slumped off, and the necessity of still further strengthening the supports of the boulder was apparent. Timbers were cut and placed under it, and when it seemed as if all was nearly secure, a great mass of gravel, earth, and snow, carrying the boulder with it, fell without a second's warning. Bud was a little farther away, and though thrown down and half buried by the stones and partially frozen earth that came on him like a wave, was not much injured. His first thought was of Zeb, who, wedged in between the fallen timbers and nearly covered by the debris, his face white as death, was almost within reach of his hands. Wildly he called out to him, but no answer came; he struggled to free himself, and at last succeeded. He could tell Zeb was still alive from his breathing; only his head and neck and one shoulder were uncovered.

Bud pulled at him, but he could not move him. He took shovel and pick, and dug and pulled the covering from him. Across his stomach and side a timber had fallen, and on one end of it was the great rock, he judged, for he could see its top, and it was in the line of the timber. With all his strength he tried to move the log, but it was not till he had loosened another from the mass where it lay half covered, that, using it as a lever, he pried the timber one side, and at last drew Zeb, unconscious, inanimate, away.

His exertions had been prodigious, and he could only gasp, "For God's sake, Zeb, dear old Zeb, are you hurt?"

Slowly the old man's senses returned, and he answered him in a dazed way. "It's all right, Jane," he said, "all right."

"Don't you know me, Zeb? It's I, Bud."

"That's so; the dang slide knocked me out. See if my legs are broken, will ye?"

No bones were broken, and very faint and pale the old man was helped to his feet.

"There's something wrong inside," he said. "I

guess my ribs are broke; and I feel weak, and I'm 'bout done up."

With great difficulty Bud brought him out of the cut, having to carry him at last, and partly dragging him on the snow-shoes, got him to the cabin, where, being more closely examined, it seemed that three ribs were broken; and bruises here and there, all over his legs and arms and body, made the accident serious enough to cause alarm.

"I don't care nothing 'bout them things if I ain't hurt inside. I kinder feel I am, but we'll tell more in a day or two," said Zeb.

Bud helped him into his bunk, and, as Zeb directed him, put such bandages around him as were necessary.

Often that night he went to the old man's bunk, finding him awake, but always deprecating so much kind attention. Next day Zeb was only able to stir about the cabin a little. There was a "bad feeling inside," as he expressed it. He insisted on Bud's leaving him and going to work as usual at the "diggins," and, as his anxiety was so marked, Bud, against his own wish, put in the day as usual, going up at noon to the cabin to see how his companion was. At night he was as cheerful as ever, displaying great interest in, and asking many questions about, what had been done that day. "I don't feel just right inside," he said; and "then perhaps I'd better keep quiet a few days on account of them ribs."

The days went by, Bud working alone, and Zeb moving about but little, and that little disapproved of by his young companion, who, so far as he could, enforced complete rest, so as to give the broken ribs a chance to unite again.

It was lonely work for the young man; he missed the cheery companionship, and it gave him more opportunity to reflect on his own trouble. He saw now that, as Zeb had said, he had, by his leaving New York, given every one the right to think he was a guilty man, and this chafed him. His remaining and holding his ground would at least have done something to convince the one of all the world he most desired to believe in his innocence. "Can it be possible," he thought, "that she will think of me as others do, as they must think of me?" And, then, there was in this lonely situation so much reason for anxiety on Zeb's account, for notwithstanding the difference in their years, education, and conditions of life, he had come to think much of the old man. "Yes," he said to himself, "you are a man, Zeb, and I love a man. What a simple, grand old character he is!" he thought. All the men he had ever known seemed so artificial beside him. Now he knew him so well, he felt he had at last met a man.

There is a certain manliness in some men that permeates the air about them; an emanation from them that neither the purple of an emperor, the fustian of a laborer, nor the buckskin of a backwoodsman can smother. It appertains neither to riches nor to poverty, to high nor lowly station. To be a man is more than to be a gentleman; to be a woman, more than to be a lady. Precept, example, education, training, surroundings, may take a passive child and make it a gentleman or a lady, provided the child be morally healthy and amiable; the graces of heart and mind under these formative agencies are built up, and, given a well-disposed, kindly child, you have as their product that consideration for others, that refinement of mind and conduct, that abhorrence of pretence, that grace and elegance of word and manner, that to our modern, broader ideas define the gentleman and lady. A man is something more, a woman is something more, than this. Man, woman, designate the male and female biped, and under these two heads all human beings of course come. We are speaking here of man at his best, of woman at her best—the ideal individuals of each sex.

There is something in the tendency of culture and gentle nurture deteriorating in its effect. No advantage is gained without some loss: it is a corollary to the law of compensation.

You may take a thoroughbred; centuries of careful breeding have made him, in most respects, an ideal horse. He has speed, courage, style, endurance, intelligence. Under easy conditions of life, everything going smoothly, good care and plenty to eat, he is as near perfection as a horse can be; but when he is placed side by side with a half-wild mustang, and has to carry his rider and accoutrements over a rough mountain country, living on its scanty grass, some days getting water, and some days going without a drop, the mustang will kill him and be none the worse for it. There is a certain horse vigor about the one that art, while it has made the other a better horse in most particulars, has deprived the thoroughbred of.

You may take a rose, a product of most painstaking and long-continued development from an original wild rose. It seems a perfect thing; its appearance, its odor, crown it queen among flowers. In its long evolution from its parent stock it has gained much, but it has lost something; the fresh, delicate wild flavor has gone.

These are both physical changes in horse and in rose, but in mankind the mental change is not less marked.

A Latin author, speaking of something to be done, says: This requires not the brawn of the athlete, but the sinew of the soldier. Brawn is the result of cultivation; the gymnasium has made it. Sinew is formed by the rough contact of man with the forces of nature; it develops under hunger and thirst; it waxes strong and tense and elastic under hardships. Brawn and sinew of heart and mind there are in a sense.

A king upon his throne may have been born with the foundation for the best development of both, and nature and art may leave him man and gentleman. A rough mountaineer may be a man, and lack but little of being a gentleman; the man is born, the gentleman is made.

There was about Zeb a virility of thought, expression, and manner; a masterful bearing in the conflict between man and the forces opposed to him when, single-handed, he contends in the wilderness for existence; a courage and determination that nothing could blunt.

A simple patriotism and love of country dominated him. A stern sense of justice, a heart as tender as a woman's, a dauntless spirit, a modesty that concealed all these until there came some puff of indignation, some breeze of sentiment, some blast of need, that swept aside the veil and showed to all about him what was behind it, gave him a charm in Bud's eyes.

Then he was so unselfish in the little matters that, where two men live alone, are all the time coming up, and so sympathetic over Bud's own troubles that his heart warmed to him as it never did to any man before.

And now this man, this friend, lay, he feared, in more danger than he would admit, or perhaps himself knew. The loneliness of their situation, their complete isolation from any chance of aid of any kind oppressed him, and with a troubled heart he did his work. Aside from an almost feverish interest in the results of the day's labor, that in much questioning and advice manifested itself nightly, Zeb continued much the same for some days.

One evening, however, as the old man lay in his bunk, and after the doings of the day had been most minutely gone over, he said, "You see them marks on the log here?" pointing to the wall at the side of his bunk. "I'm keeping my time here, Bud, and we'd better settle 'bout it now; my idee is that four dollars a day is about squar, considering everything; what do ye think? If that ain't right, say what you think would be."

"Right for what, Zeb? What do you mean?"

"Why, for the time I lay off and you're a-working."

"I don't understand what you are talking about, Zeb."

"Yer a-working more nor me, and what I want to know is what would be squar to pay you for it; and when we get the dust I'll owe you as much as them marks at so many dollars a day will come to. I'll put one down every day till I get up, if I ever do."

"Zeb, you would not owe me a dollar if you did not work for a year. I owe you so much now, more than I can ever pay. It is not dollars I owe you, it's health you have given me, Zeb; it's some sort of peace I owe you, for your trust and confidence and sympathy have done more to make my mind and heart well and strong than anything else could have done."

"Hold, Bud. That I trust ye and love ye like a son, there ain't no doubt; and that I owe ye when I don't work and ye do, there ain't no doubt on, neither. Right is right, and I want it so. I won't have it no other way."

Bud insisted that the matter should not be considered, but Zeb was obdurate.

"There's laws to all things," he said; "and though they ain't in no book, and lawyers don't know 'bout them, mebbe, they're laws, and the law among pardners is that when one don't work he pays the others, and it comes out of his sheer; mostly it's four dollars a day, but that's how they agree. It can't be no other way, Bud; it's pardners' law, and ye ain't going to go agin that, are ye? We've got to have everything regular. It can't be no other way."

"Then if that's so, I lost some days when we came back from leaving the horses."

"Of course ye did, and likely ye've got the marks for 'em somewhere."

"I never thought of it, Zeb. I didn't mark anything down, but I know it was two days, and next day I wasn't good for anything, so it's three."

"Ye was in the cut, and so ye didn't lose that day. It's pardners' law, too, that if ye've a tool in your hand at the work ye don't lose time."

Zeb was so determined about this matter that Bud had to acquiesce.

"We'll cross out two of these marks of mine, and then it will be all right;" and Zeb, as he spoke, crossed out two of the marks. "I'm going to say something to ye," he continued; "mebbe there won't be no need, mebbe there may. I'm hurt inside, Bud; I don't give nothing for them ribs, they'll be all right; but something's wrong inside of me, and I don't know how 'twill come out. It's best to make everything right when ye can, and not wait till ye can't. I give ye a letter, ye mind it, Bud, and I've got yer promise 'bout that; but there's another thing, and I'll fix that now, and then we won't talk no more 'bout it. I've got a little buckskin sack here; Yank's pipe he give me the day he was killed is in it, and there's another thing in it, and if so be I play out, which in course can happen to any man any time, I want ye to put the sack inside my shirt here," touching his heart with his hand, "when ye roll me in my blankits."

"Don't talk like that, Zeb," said Bud.

"And if it comes that way," said the old man, "I give ye my outfit, the hosses and all. Ye'll be kind to old Bally, I know ye will. He's an old devil, I know, but we've been a long time together, and you'll stand his cussedness till he dies. It won't be long, for he'll kinder miss me. He never give a damn for nobody but me. And ye'll keep the old gun; it's spoke loud and struck true for me many a time; if 'twas anybody but ye, Bud, my boy, I'd tell ye to roll it in the blankits with me."

"Why, Zeb, you will be all right in a few days, and you must not get discouraged; it's dull being here alone all day and you get blue, that's all."

"Well, Bud, mebbe it's so; but what I've said won't do no harm, and them things was on my mind."

"If you only had a doctor; if you were only where you could have care. What do you think is wrong, Zeb? How do you feel?" And Bud questioned him, and went over to him, taking his big, sinewy hand in his.

"I don't know. I don't feel right, but mebbe, as you say, I'll be all right soon. I see a feller once; he was caved on like me, and I've thought of him a hundred times sence I've been laying here. The doctor told me he had a clost call, but he fetched him out all right. I disremember what it was he give him, and if I did, course we hain't got it here; but I hain't no idee 'twas the medicine did it."

"How far do you think it is to a doctor, Zeb?"

"Must be one hundred and forty or fifty miles to Placerville. I reckon there's a doctor there, but he might as well be in heaven, if that's a place one on 'em ever goes to, which I have my doubts on. Some on 'em's good, I suppose, but they run dang thin on this coast, I tell ye.

"I hain't had no conceit of 'em sence the fall Yank and me come into Nevady. We was a-travelling along, gitting up into the mountains, and one day we stopped a while at a little town. There was an old friend of ours there and we went into his cabin and he got us dinner. I never went much on salt, but Yank he was the dangdest man for salt I ever see; there warn't none on the table, and he says to the man, 'Hain't yer any salt, Sam?' 'Yes, there 'tis on the window,' he says; and Yank reaches out and gits it. We'd finished eating, and 'twas little we had, for Sam was out of luck, when he passed long by the window. I see him grow pale. 'My God!' he says, 'Yank, ye've got the pizen,' and out he rushes for the doctor. Yank says, 'I don't taste nothin'; I don't feel nothin'.' In a minnit in comes Sam. 'Quick,' he says; 'have ye got any dust? The doctor won't come less he's a twenty.' We hadn't but a little silver. 'Where is he?' I says. 'Come 'long with me,' he says; and we go up the street two or three houses, and into the doctor's office, and a meaner looking cuss I never see. 'Come quick,' I said, 'my pardner's pizened.' 'Give me twenty,' said he. 'I hain't got it; but come, I'll give ye all we've got.' 'No, I won't go,' he says. I reached for him, and in a minnit he was afore Yank in the cabin. 'There's the man,' I said. 'He's pizened; do you fix him up. Mind ye, if Yank dies, I'll kill ye. Keep back,' I said to the few that was coming in; 'no man comes in here.' The doctor was ugly, but I meant it, and he knew it; so he sent Sam for some stuff, and Sam told them outside how it was, and they was all with me.

"Yank said he didn't feel nothing, and he says, as he took some of the stuff on his finger, 'I'll taste that agin;' and, before we could stop him, he did. 'Well,' says he, 'if that ain't salt, I'll be danged. I tell ye it's salt.' Just then Sam came in with the medicine, and going up to the tin, looked agin, and then he lifted up a board in the floor, and there was another tin. 'It's all right. I thought he'd taken the pizen, but it's here; that's salt,' he cried out.

"I was never so glad in my life. I could have cried, and hugged Yank. But warn't it singerler? I began a-cussing Sam. 'Ye ornery fool,' I said, 'won't ye never have sense to think afore ye spring such a play on a man?'

"But Yank he says, 'Sam, ye've done me a power of good; I wouldn't have missed it for nothing. There never was no sermon hit me like them words of yours.'

"I was a-going to kick the doctor out, but Yank he caught me, and wouldn't have it. 'I feel pious,' he said to the cuss, 'or I'd give ye a chance to doctor yerself for a month. Git out, for Zeb is no good company for ye now.'

"And the doctor went out, and if it hadn't been for Yank, them outside would have lynched him; as it was, that night, after we was gone, they give him notice to leave camp in twenty-four hours.

"We sold an old hoss we had for twenty-five dollars and paid the doctor his twenty, and we put the pack on one of the riding hosses, and spelled each other a walking into Nevady, and that's how I lost my grip on doctors. I laffed 'bout it as we was a-travelling, but Yank he didn't do nothing but shoot off texts for a week. 'I tell ye, Zeb,' he'd say to me, 'I see things and thought things I'd never done afore. It wer better for my soul than Ayer's pills is for ye when yer bilious;'" and as he concluded his reminiscence, the old man laughed heartily.

He was cheerful, and save his intense interest in the recounting of the way things had gone at the "diggins," and the gloating satisfaction he displayed in weighing in his hand the increasing heaviness of the sacks in which the dust was nightly put, Zeb appeared much the same. He had grown paler, and, Bud could see, much thinner. He seemed to have little inclination to get up, and there was about him the patience and gentleness that gives one such an unquiet, apprehensive feeling when he is about a sickbed. He was so cheerful and so full of pleasant talk that, as Bud's fears for him would become oppressive, some reminiscence of old days would give him such pleasure in the telling of it, and he would laugh in so light-hearted a way, Bud would think, "Surely he can't be badly injured."

But the time came when he had no appetite, could not eat, and his legs seemed to have lost their strength. They had a little flour left, and coffee and meat rounded out the commissariat, but Zeb had no taste for simple food now.

One evening Bud said, "Zeb, I've been thinking it over, and I believe I can snowshoe into Placerville or somewhere else and see a doctor, tell him just how you are, and bring back something to help you."

"No, ye won't," said Zeb. "Ye couldn't make it, and then somebody would be a-follering ye in here if they smelt the gold. No, Bud, that won't do. I have thought it over for days as how 'twas best for ye. I thought I wouldn't tell ye, but I think I will. Bud, I'm a-going to die. I know it, and it will be lonesome like for ye; but that's what I can't save ye, Bud. Ef I only could!"

"No, Zeb, no; it isn't so. You will be all right yet; I know you will."

"No, Bud, I won't. If I was on the outside, where there was a good doctor, I doubt if it would be differnt; but here I've got to hit the trail. It seems like a mean, ornery thing to do to ye, Bud, but it can't be helped; it can't be. Some day I'll go, and ye'll do what I asked ye—all them things.

"'Twill be lonesome like for ye, but ye'll keep on working and the gold will come out, lots of it. When the water is gone and ye can't work no more, ye'll go to New York. I'd a thought to make the trip with ye and stand by ye through the thing, but I can't, Bud, I can't. That worries me the worst of anything; but ye must do it alone. And, Bud, mind ye, yer young and yer keerless. Don't never go without yer gun; a man never knows when he wants it. I was a-thinking how I'd be along and take a keer of ye."

"It can't be, Zeb, it can't be!" said Bud, and still he felt in his heart it might be. "I couldn't live here without you, Zeb. Zeb, I can't lose you. You will be better; I know you will."

"Mebbe, Bud, mebbe."

That night and the next day Bud turned it over in his own mind, pro and con. If there was a chance at all for Zeb, it was to see some doctor, get him to come back with him if he would, but that he doubted, or to tell him accurately Zeb's symptoms, and there might be a chance—who knew?—that he might give him something that would save him. Could Zeb get along without him? He would walk night and day, "and in ten days I can be back, surely," he thought. "Zeb can get around a little, and I'll fill the cabin with wood, and get the food handy for him, and he might get along. I'll make it some way, I know. I believe it's the only chance, and I'll try it," he said to himself. That noon he came up to the cabin. "I don't feel like working," he said to Zeb. "I believe I'll cut some wood; I think I'll cut a big pile of it, for every night I have to shovel out the snow to get at it;" and so he did. He filled up one side of the cabin with wood and left the matches handy; he baked a lot of bread and brought a quantity of dried meat in, and put everything in as convenient reach as possible. Zeb watched him with languid interest.

"There ain't nothing lazy 'bout ye, Bud," he said; "ye quit work below, and here ye've been a-going it. 'Pears like yer doing something all the time. Yer a help to me, Bud, and yer a comfort. I hain't took to no man, 'cept Yank, like I has to you."

The snowshoes were made ready, and bread and dried meat put in an old flour sack, and matches were put in every pocket he had by Bud. He wrote in large, plain letters, telling Zeb he had gone to the doctor's; that he might depend on his being back in about ten days; that everything was put handy for him; and ended by saying: "Keep up courage, Zeb; I'll be back with something to help you soon."

Never was Zeb more cheery than on that evening. The only allusion he made to himself was a stray bit of advice to Bud about how to handle the water of the spring flood.

"I mayn't be here, and I thought I'd fix it easy for ye," he said, "so ye'd know how to do well as if I was here."

"Zeb, I can't bear to have you talk so. You will be here; you are not going to leave me," Bud would say.

"Mebbe so, mebbe so," the old man would answer. "I tell ye, Bud, we're men, and there's something for me to face; and, I'm sorry, Bud, being as we are alone here together, something for ye. It's death I'm a-runnin' up agin. It's a-being without me, it's being all alone and the lack of me on the work, that's coming to you. We've got to make the best of it, both on us. When a man gets nigh the end, it's a nateral thing for him to hate to go out of the world, and I've been a wressling with the idee every day for two weeks. I would like to see ye through that thing in New York; ye'll want a man with ye. I'd like to live till we clean up, and hate to go now; seems like desarting of ye, when ye need me, Bud; but it's got to be as it is, and I know ye'll be lonesome and all that; that part of it is hard. But it's a comfort to me that we've struck it; that ye'll send the money where I want it to go. Ye don't know what a comfort that is. Why, Bud, it's something I have been a-longing for for years; it's something I've been praying for; and when a man wants a thing like that he don't give a darn for his life 'side of it. I hain't been a pious man, God knows, but he'll see how 'twas with me; it's a dang hard life to be good in, but I hain't no real bad thing on my conscience, and I kin hold up my head afore him and take my medicine. If I kin only git to Yank, if only I kin. How do you think it is, Bud? Does a man know what's going on here after he dies?"

"I don't know, Zeb; no one does. That's all a mystery. We'll all know, sometime, but it's going to be a long time for both of us, I hope, before we do."

"Mebbe, mebbe; seems like I could see more nor I could. I see ye, Bud, making this thing of yers all right; I see ye married to the girl, and little children about ye, living as ye ought to live, where there are folks, and them folks making much of ye. Say, Bud, if ye have a boy, give him my gun when ye die, and tell him, when he's a little one, how it was with an old feller who carried it from Mexico to Allasky, and how it never spoke when it didn't have cause, and how true it talked then. Tell him 'bout Yank; ye never knew him, but ye've heerd from me. Teach him to speak the truth and to love his country and his flag. I want to think something I've told ye 'bout Yank will get into his little heart, and when the time comes that may come to him, he'll be a good soldier and foller the flag as Yank did. Larning is good for boys, but the idee of the country and the flag's the main p'int. Ye'll tell him I asked ye to give him the old gun and my blessing. And when ye marry the girl, as ye will, Bud, tell her how I knew 'twould come. Say to her, 'Old Zeb is a-chuckling to himself in his grave over it, 'cause he knows she's got a man— a man he loved.' God bless ye, my boy. Yer eddicated, and yer ways are so differnt and yer life's been so differnt, but ye made me yer equal and yer friend, and I love ye. Ye'll mind the letter and what I told ye 'bout the mine. Don't have nothing to do with no bank, but Wells, Fargo; they're sure as death. Don't let Bally's manners matter; ye'll treat him well 'cause of me, I know ye will."

And then Zeb called to mind an old frolic of Yank and himself in Yreka, and that led on to his giving an account of Yank's familiarity with the Bible. "I'd give anything if I could think of them texts he used to say; they fit into whatever come along like a ball in a gun-barrel."

Bud tried to encourage him, to make him think less positively of death, but it seemed as if he had made up his mind to it. Should he go or remain? There was a faint chance that he could do something for him by seeing a doctor. Bud could not let the chance, even if it was, as he was beginning to feel, a desperate one, slip.

As the time came for turning into his bunk he had Zeb's hand in his, and with a pathos in his voice that the knowledge of his leaving made more pathetic, he said, "Zeb, you've been the truest friend to me I have ever had; since I have been with you I have learned what a man is. Whatever comes, you'll know I am a friend who loves you and doing what a friend can. Good night, Zeb. God bless you, old man," and with a quick burst of sentiment he leaned over, and, to Zeb's astonishment, kissed him.

"Ye have curous ways, Bud," he said, "but yer a man; that's in my heart. Good night to ye."

It was not long before the old man was asleep, and very cautiously Bud moved to him and pinned to the wall, where he could not fail to see it, the paper he had written. The fire gave a little light, and the peaceful face he looked down on almost diverted him from his purpose, but he felt he must take the one chance there seemed to be.

Very noiselessly he took his revolver, its cartridge-belt, and his little sack of provisions, looked around the cabin to see that all was left as easy for Zeb to get at as possible, and went out.

The moon was in its third quarter, and it was nearly as light as day. Getting on his snowshoes, with his pole in his hand and his little sack across his shoulders, he slowly moved away from the cabin, often looking back until the trees hid it from view. He had not taken a blanket with him, for he needed to be as lightly loaded as possible, and intended at night to make a big fire and snatch what sleep he could before it.

The snow was in excellent condition and he went swiftly on. But on where? From the mountain top which Zeb and he had climbed there was in his mind a general idea of his course and where the settlements lay, but that was all. He knew he must go south and a little east, and between Bernard Mountain and Scott's Peak, in which direction Zeb, as he pointed them out, had told him lay the habitations of men. A sense of the difficulty of the task he had set himself to do came to him more forcibly than ever before, but his was no heart to falter. He was young and strong, of a hardy constitution and powerful muscular frame, which the life he had led the past six months had strengthened and developed; then he had acquired an aptness on snowshoes, but, better than all, the stimulus of love for Zeb and the hope of saving his life nerved him. A hundred and fifty miles as we ride it on an express train seems a short distance, but through an uninhabited country, with snow from five to twenty feet deep covering it, with no shelter, nothing to eat or use but what one carries on his back, with great mountain divides to cross, it is another thing, quite another thing, when it is to be travelled alone.

To a man experienced in such a way of travelling, who knows the trail as you do the way to your business or to your neighbors, such a trip is no light one, and such a man would attempt it only under some such incentive as urged Bud to it. But here was a young fellow, strong and active, it is true, but lacking in the endurance which comes only from the strains such trips give, only a few months from the city, ignorant of all save the general course he was to go. Few men, perhaps, ever took part in a more forlorn hope; with him, however, there was that blissful ignorance of its difficulties that, after all, is an element of success in many undertakings. True, he knew it was a difficult thing to do, but how difficult and how desperate he could not know.

Before sunrise he had climbed and crossed the divide that made the rim of the basin. The moon made the two far-away peaks discernible, and between them his way lay. In the early morning light he sped down from the summit where he had stopped to fix clearly in his mind the track he was to follow. The cañon made by the river lay along his way; he would follow along it. After sunrise he stopped a bit and ate some bread and dried meat. All that day he pushed on over a country of low, broken hills, with occasionally a little valley and a higher hill to climb and ride down on his snowshoes. Before night he stopped where an abundance of dry timber, fallen here and there, with the tops of the dried black pines caught against some living tree, gave fuel for his fire. He had not encumbered himself with an axe, and had to depend on breaking, by main strength, branches and the smaller pieces of wood, or putting on bodily the logs he could drag up and let the fire burn them in two. He had his big knife, to use in making the fire. He made a great blaze, and drew before it two logs as large as he could master, on which he could sit or lie out of the snow and rest, if he could not sleep. He munched his bread and jerked venison, and waited for the long night to pass. He determined, if the weather remained clear, to use the night for travelling, and rest when the sun was up; for the chilliness of the air went through him, and his clothes, damp from perspiration, made him shiver when he turned from the fire. He was tired and sore, for he had, he calculated, been fully nineteen hours on his snowshoes, but he was pleased with his progress; he must have gone over two miles an hour, he thought; but to be sure he put it at forty miles, though he felt he had probably made nearer fifty. At any rate, he was very tired, and fell into fitful slumbers, from which he would wake half frozen, and make the fire blaze up again, and warm himself at it, and then doze off again; so a long night passed, and the break of dawn was pleasant to his eyes, and, better still, the rising of the sun in its clear winter glory. It was hardly sunrise, though, before he was on his way again.

That day he walked until afternoon, a little stiffly at first, but soon his old swing came back to him, and he thought, when he stopped to make a fire, that he had gone fifteen miles or so, and probably sixty since he had started.

He made his fire and ate the little portion he had in his mind as a proper division of what he had, and lying down in the warm sun, with the fire adding to the heat, he slept a few hours, until the chilliness of evening roused him.

In a way, the ground he had gone over was, to a certain extent, familiar to him, for over much the same course had Zeb and he come from Cape Horn when they entered the Yellow Pine Basin; and though he could by no means follow the way they had come, so much did the deep snow change the appearance of the country, yet here and there he recognized familiar objects in some rounded hill or great upturned rock; and in a general way the river, which he was going up, would, he knew, bring him to Cape Horn. There were cabins—there might be men in them—perhaps twenty miles from there, towards Stanley, but there was no doctor there, nor for a long distance beyond, and it was very doubtful if there was any one at the cabins, and he felt he could not risk going there. At the settlements he had started for, Zeb had said there were doctors, and there he determined to go. The moon still gave him light, though clouds were coming up, but they by no means obscured it, and the snow was still hard. That night he had made good headway, though he was beginning to feel the wear of the walk and suffered from lack of sleep; his broken and uneasy slumbers, for he could only doze an hour or two at a time, gave him little rest, but the absorbing importance of his mission kept him on his weary walk.

When morning came he was nearing Cape Horn, and when the sun rose he stopped for rest near where Cape Horn Creek meets that other, then nameless, one, which rises near the summit of the Bear Valley divide, and, uniting with it, pours its waters into the Salmon below.

On the hillside above him came from out of the snow a rough-hewn plank, showing a foot or two of its end, and marking, as he knew, for Zeb had told him of it, the grave of a man killed in some Indian skirmish but a year or two before, one of those perishable mementoes of the lives that have been lost in the long fight that has won to peace and growing civilization our western empire. On hill and in valley sleep those who fell; crumbling, unsubstantial tombstones have some, others none; but to them rises up an ever-growing monument, its foundations, constitutions of States; the great blocks above them, laws of prosperous commonwealths laid in the cement of justice to all, of peace, of good will; the years adding to its towering height, till, in the fulness of time, shall crown it all some figure emblematic of that perfect man whom the millennium will find upon the earth.

Making a fire and eating his meagre breakfast, bringing up before the fire some logs that he might stretch himself upon, took little time, and Bud was soon taking such sleep as the hardness of his bed allowed.

That all roads led to Rome was a feature in the old world travel; no less positive a one in that portion of Idaho we are speaking of is that all roads lead to Cape Horn. Does a man desire to go anywhere, the mountain ranges converge his trails to Cape Horn, for there is the best pass in all the mountains.

To the west of it lies Bear Valley, separated from it by some twelve miles or so of distance, and by only a moderate rise of divide. Crossing into the valley, which, like a clover leaf, is divided into three parts, and going up the easterly division, along a tributary of the Salmon, you travel some fifteen miles or so until, by an almost imperceptible rise from that side, you go down to the waters of the Deadwood. To the right of this is Bernard Mountain, so called after a gallant officer who, a year or two before the time we are speaking of, led an expedition against the Indians, then troublesome in the country to the north; and away to the south of it looms up Scott's Peak, its name the only memorial of an early pioneer, the highest mountain in the high, steep range across the Deadwood. Beyond this range somewhere was our snowshoer's destination.

The sun now, as the months of spring in more favored localities were near at hand, was higher in the heavens, and a mildness in the air, through which its rays came down upon the sleeping man, helped out the hard bed the logs on which he lay made, and gave him more restful sleep than he had yet had, and it was well towards sundown when the uneasy turnings his rough couch caused him to make were disturbing enough to awaken him.

He doled out to himself his prescribed ration of bread and jerked meat, and taking a drink of water, Bud began again his monotonous tramp. Under the genial sun and in the warm air the snow had softened, and laboriously he plodded on, his shoes clogging and sinking deeply. It was well along in the night when he crossed the divide into Bear Valley and experienced the delightful sensation of being helped by his shoes, instead of retarded, as he went down hill. Towards morning the snow became a little hard again. Aided by the light from the now only occasionally perceptible moon, he directed his course towards the point where its light had shown him, from the divide, the mountain range in which seemed to lie the two peaks his way should lead between; and through the flat valley, which had gradually narrowed, and beside a stream which, frozen over here and there, sluggishly traversed it, he made his way with weary body but stout heart. If he could only get back in time; if he could only bring some relief; if there was anything that could relieve! At times the snow would be hard enough to bear him, and then he would sink in it a few inches, but still, with unconquerable determination, with unfaltering, persistent stride, he slowly put the miles behind him.

As morning neared, the snow was stiffer, and he made up his mind to plod along until the sun of another day should soften it. With machine-like regularity he moved his legs, sliding the shoes along, counting their movements as he might the swinging pendulum of some great clock, and checking off each hundred steps upon his fingers. Dawn came, and the machine was working; the sun rose, and still the measured swing of leg kept on, and hot fell the solar beams before was turned off from it the steam of the strong will that had made Bud's numbed limbs respond to its impelling force as does steel shaft in the engines made in shops to the vapors of water.

He had now been out three days and more, and it was with delight that he saw Bernard Mountain to the right and nearly even with him; Scott's Peak he could see also, and between them, right in his course, the Deadwood Range, across which his way lay. He made his fire well down from the divide, towards the Deadwood.

Fortunately, when he awoke from his sleep, a growing coldness in the air and a clear sky indicated that the storm he had dreaded had gone by, and bespoke for him better travelling. He rose very weary, but his goal seemed nearing, and with a lighter heart he again began his tramp.

In some ten miles or thereabouts he crossed the Deadwood where it ran slowly and the ice had bridged it, and began the toilsome climbing of the mountain that to the south of it separated such settlements as there then were from the wilderness through which he had come. The snow was hard, not with that solid, icy hardness that makes ascent tedious from the slipping back of the shoes, but hard enough to sustain them, with only enough of sinking to keep them from slipping. A new strength had come to him; he was on the last forty miles, he knew, and only forty miles away lay Zeb's possible salvation; now it was thirty-nine, and now it was thirty-eight, and though steep and rough was the way, his rising spirits gave vim and vigor to him. By early morning he was on the divide, and the fast-coming light saw him riding on his shoes with the speed of the wind, decreasing the distance before him as the long downward stretches gave him opportunity, and climbing again some small rise that raised the grade, which, from the summit of these mountains, drops to the south fork of the Payette, almost three thousand feet, in a little over twenty miles. By noon the fork of the Payette lay before him, only a few miles away, and by two o'clock he was on its bank and searching for solid ice to cross on; this he found, and up into the quickly rising ground from it he went.

CHAPTER XI

A HIGH range of hills encircles with its rim the Boise Basin, in which lie Idaho City, Centreville, and Placerville, centres for trade and traffic of the region about them. In them are dwelling-houses, China shacks, saloons, gambling-houses, mercantile establishments, and such other structures as the needs, virtues, and vices of their indwellers demand. Law and Medicine represent there the learned professions, the Church only intermittingly venturing into the field, and groping with irresolute and vacillating endeavors after the souls whose earthly forms serve in its traffic, support its saloons, or through the long winter are lined up against the big stoves that warm the resorts of sale and barter or the temples of Bacchus. Much given are the winter frequenters of these towns to tales of their own valor in the past, and to reminiscences of glorious bygone times when gold was to be had, it seems, for the mere picking up of the nuggets; sinking deep shafts, running great tunnels, building great ditches, in their minds, that, when the working season comes, will have melted away as has the snow that clogs the streets.

The virtues of such centres are their own, and they are strong and many; their follies have either an amusing or a pitiful side, and the sum of them all is expressed in such good-natured, hearty good will and helpfulness for all physical suffering, that whoever has not a warm place in his heart for the dwellers in them knows them not.

The stores had closed, and the more domestic and home-loving population of Placerville were asleep. On three sides of the Plaza, which occupies the centre of the little town, the light streamed from the saloon windows, where were going on faro and poker, jigger, and the other games of cards which serve to circulate for a time the loose money of the community among the votaries of chance and the temporary believers in their own skill or luck, and which, when spring comes, have it all securely stowed away in the safes of the saloon keepers.

There was hard drinking and rough words, with many an oath, in one of them, when, at the top of their speed, came two foaming horses, dragging a sleigh in which were two men, one driving, the other half lying in the bottom. The noise of the sleigh and its panting horses brought all to the door, save some keen gamblers, who, at one or the other of the green baize-covered tables in the big room, were too much absorbed in their game to even turn their heads.

"What's up, Joe?" said the first one out.

"I've got a man here all beat out and wants to see the doctor. His pardner's sick somewhere in the mountains on Salmon, and he's come in for medicine; he's 'bout give out himself. Here, some of ye help me in with him."

But Bud, for it was he, needed little help, and came into the great room, the centre of a crowd of sympathizing friends. These men took in the situation at a glance. They knew where the mountains "on Salmon" were, and the long miles away they were; they knew the toil it was to come from them; they felt the strength of the tie that made this young fellow take such a trip for his partner, and one look at him, as worn and stiff he stood among them, waked the gentleness and sympathy which, deep down in the natures of such men, but needs some like cause to bring it to the surface.

"Sit down here. Bring the man some whiskey, can't ye?" roared out the deep voice of the saloon-keeper to the man behind the bar. "Put some wood in, Link, and start up the fire. Down with the whiskey and warm up," he said to Bud; "you had a long trip, hadn't ye?" This one asked him if his boots had better not come off, and started to pull them; and another ran to his cabin and came back with a great pile of cold beans on a tin plate, insisting he must eat; while a giant of a man ordered the bar-keeper to bring cigars; and all with ready sympathy stood around him, asking no questions, but evidently waiting for him to speak.

The driver had put up his horses and came in, and up to the bar, after seeing that Bud was being properly attended to.

"Leave him alone," he said. "He's dead for sleep, and the whiskey and the fire will do him good;" and as he spoke, Bud dropped into a slumber.

As they all ranged up against the bar, Joe Ladd, a rancher in a valley twelve miles away, told his story.

"I was up the hill, 'cross Alder Creek, looking out a tree to make shakes, and see this feller coming along; he was some ways off, but soon as I see him I knew he was beat out. He'd push the shoes, and then he'd stop and almost fall down, and then he'd plug along, and he fell, but he got up agin, and he had hard work to do it. I ran down to him, and he says, 'Where is Placerville, and is there a doctor there?'

"He said his partner was sick; he was come to see a doctor and get something for him. He was clean give out, and said he'd come one hundred and fifty miles, and way below Cape Horn. I helped him along, for he was about snow-blind, and got him down to the cabin. 'Take me to the doctor,' he says; 'I must see him.' I wanted him to lay over till morning, but he said every hour counted, so I hitched up the horses and brought him in here."

The doctor had been aroused by some one, and came in just as Bud woke up. The stimulant and his short sleep had a little refreshed him, and he told the doctor the circumstances of Zeb's injury, and gave as accurate an account of his symptoms as possible, answering the kind and searching questions of the doctor as best he could.

"From what you say," said the medical man, "there may be any one of several internal injuries, and all of them are bad; most of them fatal in time. There is a chance, however, that by proper keeping up of his strength, and so giving nature a show, he may pull through; it's only a chance, though."

"Can't you come back with me and see him?" said Bud.

"I couldn't do that," the doctor said. "I never was on snowshoes, and I never could make it. I ain't a hearty man, and it would be the death of me. No, I can't go."

"I'd pay you anything, doctor. I haven't got much

here, but I've some money in the bank, and I've got a gold watch here, and I've got a good claim, and so has Zeb, my partner."

"It's not to be thought of. I'm sorry I can't, but I could never stand it;" and his weak physique told Bud plainly that it was so.

"Then, doctor, give me what you can, for I must go back in the morning."

"You can't do that, man; you are weak, and you are blind nearly. You must rest up a bit, or you'll never make it."

"I shall go in the morning, doctor," said Bud. "I couldn't rest and Zeb dying; every minute is of importance. I'm going."

All tried to dissuade him, but to no purpose.

A little knot of men had gathered in a corner, and among them Joe the rancher.

"Fix up your stuff, doctor," he said. "Some of the boys and me has made it up. We'll leave here along late tomorrow, and I'll carry him and Jack Sinclair and Bill Strong in the sleigh up as far as I can, and Bill and Jack will help him on a piece, may be to the Deadwood; top of the divide, any way. The snow will be hard by the time he'll have to snowshoe."

The doctor put a poultice of raw potatoes on Bud's eyes, which now pained him intolerably, and promised to make up such medicines as might do Zeb some good. Bud was put to bed, and soon the town was still.

The next day Bud's eyes were very bad, but the pain had gone; he could barely see, however. The story had gotten over the little community, and all were interested. The watch vendor, who styled himself, in black letters on a big white sign that strung itself across the front of his modest shop, "watchmaker and jeweller," a sour, crabbed man, unsocial and repelling, came into the saloon where Bud sat by the fire, and putting in his hand a pair of snow-glasses, said, "Take them; they'll help you;" and darted out again as if afraid he might repent of his generosity if he stopped a second, closing the door to a chorus of "I'll be dang'd!" and "Bless me!" from the observers, who had never seen such a side to him. The landlady of the hotel gave her kindly heart the rein and killed some chickens, which her Chinese cook roasted, and these, with various other dainties, she sent to Bud. Old Hock Harris left his accustomed seat before the great stove in the brick store, and forced on him part of a bottle of what he told him was "the likeliest thing he ever see for a man was caved on;" a box of cigars and bottles of whiskey came from the other saloons, and advice was volunteered him by almost every one.

The big store-keeper sent word to him to come in and take what he wanted, and the principal gambler of the place appeared with the most expensive pair of boots money would buy, and gave them to him, while a natty faro dealer insisted on his donning a new thirty-dollar suit at his expense. Even Sam Sing, the boss Chinaman, came in with half a dozen green "china plasters," which he said were in such a case "heap good."

The kindness of all touched Bud. He tried to restrain this unlooked for and unnecessary liberality, but soon seeing it would be matter of offence if he refused any thing, the green table near him was covered with ever augmenting evidences of that touching of the popular heart which in like communities the sufferings and necessities of the veriest stranger produces.

He could pay for nothing. "Yer money ain't good here," was the way all, even the doctor, put it; and he could only thank, with warm heart, the kindly folks who bade him "Good-by" and "Good luck for ye," as, after noon, Joe and his two friends started away with him in the sleigh.

Having, fortunately for him, not subjected himself to the glare of the sun on the snow, except on the last day, Bud's eyes, though weak and hardly of any use to him, had not been so badly hurt as to bring on a severe case of snow-blindness, and they had already begun to mend, for he had kept them closed under his new snow-glasses as they rode along.

The ride, for he was comfortably seated, seemed to rest him, and when in the early evening the horses had brought them as far as they could, some sixteen miles from Placerville, he felt better than he had expected, and ready to try the snowshoes again, his body somewhat strained and weary, but his heart cheered by the helpful spirit of all he had met, and with the hope of relief he had for Zeb.

He could not carry a tenth of the many things that had been forced on him and which were in the sleigh. The doctor's medicines, a bottle of whiskey, some of the provisions, and the coat of the suit he took, leaving the other things with an injunction to the good-natured rancher to take care of them. Jack and Bill, his companions, thinking it was necessary, took a bottle of whiskey each, and some of the provisions.

With the best wishes of Joe Ladd, the trio started; his new friends insisted on carrying his load, and in single file, Jack Sinclair in the lead, they began to climb into the mountains.

Both of his companions were hardy mountaineers, but the winter's rest and dissipation had added fat to their frames, and, even worn as he was, Bud was better on the shoes, so that aside from their taking his load, and their company, he was rather retarded than helped by them; however, if they held him back, the somewhat slow and deliberate progress made drew less on the reserve of strength he had.

Morning found them well over the divide, and Bud insisted that there was no need of their keeping on farther, and somewhat reluctantly the kind-hearted fellows parted with him. Taking his load and thanking them for their well-meant exertions, he took the down grade towards the Deadwood.

A few miles farther on he made his fire, and, eating something, curled up on the logs and slept, starting again as night came on. All that night he plodded on. It was getting warmer, and the snow was soft, making progress very difficult. He struck his old tracks and they encouraged him, for they led where he was going, and seemed to connect him with Zeb. "If I can only get to him in time; if I can only bring some help to him," he thought; but there had been that in what the doctor said, and in the way he said it, that told him how desperate he thought Zeb's case was, and it grieved him to the heart and filled his mind with apprehension, though it no whit diminished his persistence. He had often to stop, and the consciousness came over him of waning strength; but if his legs were weary and his back and thigh muscles sore and stiff, his heart was strong, and through the clogging snow and up the rising ground he pushed his shoes.

The night was overcast, masses of clouds gathering, through which the moon, now full, as it came up, only at times shone faintly out; there was a storm brewing, and that added to Bud's intense eagerness to go on. Morning found him only just over the divide, into Bear Valley, and there he felt he must stop to rest. He awoke after a few hours' sleep, and though it was still long to sundown, he started on his way. He ran in his old track, for there the snow was harder, but it was slow, tedious work; before night came he stopped again where Elk Creek, coming from the south, joins the Bear Valley stream, and rested an hour or more, and then at it again.

Night shut down with thickening clouds all over the heavens, and there came a gentle sighing of a wind that he felt would in time bring up the storm he feared. There was no moon all night; the sickly haze of light as it rose indicated that it was above the clouds; but no sight of the round orb came to cheer him. All night he dragged along. He would stop and get his breath, for the exertion was great, and when a little chilly from his damp clothes, for they were steaming from the perspiration his efforts caused, he would start again and monotonously stride on. He felt he must not stop, and so into the next morning the shoes ploughed on. At Cape Horn he stopped, weary beyond belief, lighted his fire, and threw himself down for fitful and little restful sleep.

That day the clouds broke and at night came a little frost; the snow stiffened, and in his old track he walked with less fatigue than before, making good headway, and cheered in spite of his wasting strength by the thought he was nearing Zeb.

In two more days he would be with him to save him if there was salvation for him, to care for him if there was not. But there came with morning another change; the dark lines of clouds, repulsed in their first attack, came now in better order, well closed up, like an army which, marching on in scattered and unprepared condition, is driven back by some temporary and unexpected onset of its foes, but when the surprise is over reforms its disciplined battalions into lines of battle as solid and orderly as they seem irresistible.

So were the forces of the storm moving on, every gap filled, great solid masses. All day, as the tired man slept, were new divisions, heavier batteries massed, and when Bud woke the light skirmishing had begun. He brushed the snow from him; every hour was precious now, and, nerved by the new obstacle, he jumped on his shoes, and eating his bread and meat as he walked, pushed on.

Of all the contests man wages with the elements, none is more appalling than when a snow-storm in the mountains meets one in some such condition of strength as Bud then was, whose knowledge of the way is as superficial as was his. Besides the retarding effects of accumulating snow there comes this serious, often deadly, effect: The vision, limited to a few yards, distorted and uncertain as it peers through the falling snow, can get no familiar object in its short range; and even if one there should be, so changes its appearance that one fails to recognize it, or thinks he sees some remembered rock or tree, and, lured by it, turns aside to wander in labyrinths of alternate hope and despair, until exhausted he sinks a victim to the ruthless, inexorable tempest.

Bud knew this, but while his tracks could be traced there was no danger, for they led back to the cabin, and some depth of snow would have to fall to entirely obliterate them; still it was a danger which required him to strain every nerve to get as far along as he could before the track was gone. At first the flakes came scattered and hesitatingly, but they grew more frequent as the evening came on, and settled down at last to a steady fall.

As hour after hour passed and the depth of snow increased, the pace which Bud had taken and kept, particularly as his way was now up and down over the ridges and depressions which mark in every mountain country the incoming of tributaries into a main stream, began to exhaust him. The necessity of using each hour to the best advantage sustained him in a degree, however, and he kept on with the same dogged perseverance that had so long animated him.

As day came, many inches of snow covered his old snowshoe marks, and it was now more rapidly nearing the time when they would quite disappear. His mind concentrated itself on one thing, the getting to Zeb as quickly as he could.

When morning fully broke he was, he judged, only thirty miles away from the cabin, but the growing difficulties of the impeding snow, and the certainty that soon the lines marking the old tracks beneath would no longer be a guide to him, caused his stout heart to feel more apprehension than ever before.

He would not stop so long as he could trace the course, and not until the blank white surface before him was unbroken by a single indication of the trail it concealed, and until even it was no longer to be seen now and then faintly discernible under trees where the snow, warded off by the overhanging boughs, fell less deeply, did he stop to take a needed rest and to prepare for what he knew was to be a hard fight for his own life as well as Zeb's.

He made a fire with difficulty, the snow having dampened such dry wood as he could find; he ate almost the last of his provisions and laid himself down to some such sleep as awaits the man whose mind is prepared for its being his last, save that long one we must all some time take. But exhaustion, and perhaps something of that desperation whose benumbing effect brings oblivion to the criminal on the night before his execution, gave Bud sleep, and he waked somewhat refreshed, to make that test of endurance and courage than which no sterner ever comes to man.

He went over in his mind the way he must take; he called up every tree whose appearance was different from its fellows; every marked rock, every little rise and fall of ground he could think of that might serve either as a signboard to direct him on the road, or as a confirmation of his position. One thing he knew, he must keep along the river at such distance from it as might be, as there was in that some guide.

He must leave that course and strike up to the left to cross the divide into Yellow Pine Basin, and there he felt would come the crisis; should he turn too soon, he might wander into a maze of rough country where he would unconsciously pass the heads of the little streams that, winding through the basin, seek the river; should he go too far before turning, he might miss the basin altogether, only skirting its side. He thought he could in time find the cabin, even then, but time meant Zeb's life, probably, as well as his own, for he felt he was nearing the limit of his powers.

Try as he might, he could not recall any object that in such a bewildering storm as was then raging would be near enough for him to see, and which would indicate when he was to turn aside. For ten miles or more he felt he could keep the way; beyond that, unless Providence or fortune should interpose, his mission would be a failure, and his life but another one of the long list whom the storms of earth have swept to death.

Tightening his belt, nerving his spirit, he slipped on his shoes. Now had come his last weary march; was it to lead to the little cabin, where, weak, and he felt now almost despairing, Zeb patiently awaited his coming with the balm of health, for now that ever reaching him was so doubtful, the doctor's compounds seemed of magic, unquestionable virtue; or was it to end on some storm-swept hillside, where his bleaching bones would in time crumble into nothingness and his memory only be, in the minds of those he most loved, a mystery as to whether he had been thief or honest man?

To high spirits there comes with danger, and probably approaching death, a clearness of the faculties, a command, physical and mental, of themselves, that awakes latent strength of muscle, gives sinew new elasticity and tenseness, and puts mind to its highest.

There was safety for himself, almost surely, if he

would stop, husbanding his little stock of provisions, till such time as the storm would be over, but that never came to Bud; he was too loyal to his friend to desert him in his need, even though he knew death stood between them. With loyalty that deviated not, with courage that was unfaltering in the desperate strait he was himself in, Bud left his camp.

The storm was furious, and the snow in blinding sheets shut out any object a hundred feet away; without cessation or break came down the white flakes, like cotton particles, weaving, as they touched the earth, a great winding-sheet that seemed ready, yes, hungry, to enfold him. Such trees as through this film his eyes could see, white covered, like the marble monuments in a cemetery, gave such ghostly sameness to the way, that the stout heart seemed to walk with death's banners at his side through long avenues leading to where his dreaded foe, lance in rest, awaited him.

Bud had, as I have said, something to direct him; for though at a distance above and away from it, the river was in the course he was to take. With all his failing strength he ploughed his way through the soft, new-fallen snow, going too high here and too low there, and so adding to the distance by his blundering path, but he went on. Little it mattered now whether day or night surrounded him, for any guidance he might have. The night was nearly over when he had to come to a decision to turn into the mountains. Should he turn now? No, he would go on farther, for he thought he had better make sure of not turning too soon, even if he might go too low. But at last he was sure he had gone down far enough, and stopping a few minutes for breath, and as far as possible to satisfy himself that he was right, he changed his course and struck up into the hills.

The ascent was steep; over two feet of new snow had fallen since the storm began, and Bud sank so deeply in it that movement was very difficult; he could only go a few feet at a time, his long-continued exertions had so weakened him. He took off his shoes and wallowed through the snow, carrying them; on hands and knees he burrowed along. He put the shoes on again, straining like some good swimmer nearly exhausted, but still combating an adverse current, hardly gaining distance as it seemed to him, but yet gaining.

Work against it as he might, there was creeping over him a numbness of the legs, a stiffening of his back and thigh muscles, and, worst of all, a suspicion that his mind was beginning to wander. Old scenes came to him—trifling, long-forgotten incidents of his childhood; his bitter experience in New York; a fair face, now a little fond, now changed as doubt and suspicion moulded its plastic and expressive features; Zeb's peril—all with panoramic movement passed before him. With an effort of will he tried to fix his mind on one thing, Zeb's waiting, patient face, and concentrated his attention on the little cabin, the goal of his strivings. He went over every detail of its homely architecture, every interior fitting in its rude appointments—the great fireplace, Zeb's bunk with its wan, weak occupant.

"I will," he said, "go there; the demons of the storm shall not hold me back. I will keep my senses; I am coming, Zeb;" and then, with a spurt of energy and strength, he would gain a little distance, till, from very inability, he would have to stop and breathe. Then would come over him a torpor of both mind and body, with an almost irresistible impulse to throw himself down. He knew if he did he would sink into sleep, and with all the powers of a mind naturally strong, and an absorbing, overmastering devotion to his friend, he combated the desire. He would start, to stop and go over it all again.

Noon came and passed, and with tenacity of purpose, holding before his eyes the cabin, brushing aside the ever-gathering legions of sirens that would lull him to stop and rest, his will power contracting and expanding his muscles, he moved on. No longer had he strength, no longer vigor of body; matter was exhausted, mind sustained him.

At last he reached the summit, but he did not stop; down the hill he walked, slid, staggered, but on always; with all the resolution he had he kept the one thing before him.

He could not recognize an object he had ever seen; he doubted if his course was right, but now he had no choice; the little strength that was in him must be spent in going on. If he was wrong, all was gone—Zeb's life, his. It was a desperate chance, but it was the only one. Night came, and stumbling up and down, erratic, waving from side to side, he went on. The fancies of delirium came to him; but like a fine, hot sun his singleness of purpose, his unconquerable determination, every now and then broke through the clouds and mists that passed athwart his mind, and were as light to his path.

Fantastic shapes the snow-laden trees assumed—tombs of past pleasures, palaces of new ones yet to come; dead faces, living ones; but behind him, as he turned, ever two fiery lights that seemed to follow, keeping pace with him, not twinkling stars, but fixed, steady, horrible in their persistence. Once he fancied he heard a growl; but was it only a false note in the strains of music, gay, pensive, sombre, that rang in his ears as the sirens sang? At last his benumbed faculties gave reality to these following, stalking lights; a cougar was on his path, biding its time till weak from fatigue he should drop and be his prey.

He laughed; what dread had he of beast when the air was full of gathering ghastly angels of death, and those of fairer form who, under guise of soft blandishments, were wooing him to restful annihilation?

His spirits rose. "Beasts or devils, I am coming, Zeb! I am coming," he said, he shouted, and through the snow he wound his uncertain, staggering way. But now the foe was on him. Delirium held him, perched on his shoulders, her tightening, fateful fingers clutching at his throat. All feeling of consciousness was gone, but still was left that other power mind has in dire extremity to work its unseen will on senses slumbering meanwhile. Even with more directness, even with more vigor than before, went on the body, while in a thousand wayside paths strayed off Bud's wandering senses.

He knew nothing more—in after years he could recall nothing more—until, standing before a stump from which the axe had cut the tree, a ray of light, flickering, but light, stole into his mind.

"Thank God!" he thought, "it's the snowshoe tree Zeb cut;" and off he started from it, true as an arrow, to the cabin, his mind cleared from all illusions.

He left his shoes before the canvas door and stumbled into the cabin. "Zeb, I am here. Zeb," he called. No answer came, and there was no fire; an awful silence was there. Uncertain, trembling, he made his way through the darkness to Zeb's bunk, and put out a questioning hand as cold as the still face his fingers touched.

"Dead! dead!" he said, and fell unconscious on the floor.

CHAPTER XII

Through the canvas at the door and the cracks between the logs of the cabin, daylight came filtering in. Dazed and wandering, Bud awoke from the sleep of exhaustion and the shock of the great sorrow and calamity that had come to him; awoke as one from a troubled dream, and slowly collected his senses. He was in the cabin, he saw, and then memory came back, and painfully, slowly rising, every muscle aching, stiff and worn and faint, he stood up and looked on all that was left of his friend. He moved away and sank into the chair on which lay the monster skin of the silver tip, his elbows on his knees, and his face buried in his hands.

Weakened as he was by the terrible and long-continued strain of the last ten days, lack of food and sleep, now that the stimulus of hope was gone, making him weaker still, he burst into a flood of tears. "Too late! Too late!" he sobbed, and then the awful loneliness of his position came to him and quieted him. He had much to do, and he must do it. Weak as he was, he must do what was to be done alone.

When the first burst of irrepressible sorrow had passed, Bud made a fire, and drank and ate to put the strength in him he felt was so greatly needed, and then before the warm fire he dropped asleep again. An hour or two he slept, and woke clearer in mind, but so lame and weak that he could hardly move.

Zeb lay as death had found him. His peaceful face told how quietly and gently the bold spirit had parted from the weak, scarred frame it had animated. One hand lay on his heart, clutching a faded, crumpled piece of blue ribbon; the other, by his side, had its dead fingers holding the little buckskin sack he had in life so greatly prized; on the bed was the Testament he had kept on his shelf.

The tears came in Bud's eyes; his heart was heavy as over the lifeless clay he recalled the sterling virtues of the man, and felt the void his death must make. But there pressed on him, even as he looked, the necessities that death involves, and he turned away to consider how he might, in his loneliness and solitude, do such decent and fitting putting away of what remained to claim his sorrowful and tender care as time and place allowed.

On the table, in the litter that told of Zeb's having taken bread and drink, lay evidences of a somewhat recent movement, and as his eye took in the crusts and crumbs and half-empty tin cup, he saw his name in big, wandering letters on a folded paper. He took it up, and opening it, read:

"For all ye done, Bud, I thank ye, but it's no good. I'm a-going, and I can't wait no ten days; 'twouldn't be no good, ennyway. I'm called, and I've got to go.

"I orter told ye mor'n I did, but ye send the letter to Jim Peasley, and the money; he'll know where it's to go. Don't ye be a-lonely nor afeered; jes' think I'm gone. Wrap me in my blankits, with the sack I tol' ye in my shirt, and put me under the p'int, nigh the claim. There was never no man, Bud, I took to as I has to ye, 'cept Yank.

"When ye gits the dust, go to New York and fight that thing out. Be keerful 'bout yer gun; have it where ye can draw handy and quick. I can't give ye no advice like that; always keep yer gun handy. Git one of them Smith & Wesson's six-inch barrels; I got great conceit on 'em. Keep my old gun and give it to the little feller we was a-talking 'bout. He'll come, I know he will, and ye'll be happy, and ye'll be a considerabel man, I see ye will. Don't let old Bally have no grain, never; it ain't no good for him. Take some dust outen my sheer, and put him where he'll have good grass and water, and hay in winter, long's he lives.

"'Twas a foolish thing yer going to the doctor's, and I'm afeered for ye, Bud; but I leeves ye where I am, in the hands of God, and I prays he'll see to you in the snow and the storm.

"I hain't no feer. What comes I'll take it, and if so be I'll be with Yank. I don't ask no more.

"Bud, my boy, my boy, I'm a-desartin' of ye, but I can't help it.

"Let the little feller grow up to love his country and the flag. Tell him 'bout Yank.

"Eddication's good, but the idee of the country and the flag, that's the main p'int.

"Tell her I would ha' liked to see her putty face and the children, and that I said as how 'twould come out right. Be a kind o' soft and easy with her, Bud; wimmin ain't like men.

"O Bud, I hates to leeve ye, but it's jes' got to be so. When ye go to catch Bally, take some salt, and he'll come to ye. Tell the old cuss I'm gone; he'll know. He's got the dangdest sence of any hoss I ever see.

"Ye'll do all these things, Bud.

"Don't ye have no feer of me when I'm in the ground. I'll stay thar.

"Do the best ye can, and mind yer gun, Bud. The

love I has for ye, boy, makes it a hard thing, Bud, but we mus' stan' it. Don't ye take it to heart. I ain't in no wise a-crawlin'. So far as I go, 'cept for ye, I ain't no ways sorry. Good-by. God bless ye, Bud, my boy.

"ZEB."

With what effort and laborious care this was written, it's straggling, uncertain lines gave proof. From its rude letters and expressions shone out the kindly heart, the courage that went down to death unruffled by a fear.

"God, in his infinite mercy," he said, "judge you, Zeb. Surely the spirit must be more than the letter of the law, and as your light was, so you kept it."

But there was that to be done he dreaded, but must do, and with tender, caressing hands he straightened the old man's limbs as best he could.

On his heart, under his hand and the ribbon it held, was pinned what he had never seen on him before, the eagle and the colors, the insignia of the Grand Army, and Bud thought to himself that never had it lain over heart more loyal, or evidenced more faithful and devoted service to the land whose safety and whose glory was to the old man a religion.

He took from his fingers the buckskin sack, its open mouth giving a glimpse of a scrap of frayed bunting and the end of a short clay pipe. The one he remembered as a piece of the old flag Yank had died with, and that Zeb had afterwards so lovingly borne; the other, as Yank's pipe he had given him just before the battle, as Zeb had told him.

When all was ready, Bud put the little sack on his breast, under the coarse woollen shirt he had replaced on him, for he would not remove from it the badge Zeb's almost dying hands must have pinned there. The ribbon his hand held he left there, and the hand he replaced as he had found it. Reverently he wound Zeb's blankets around him, and, when all was done, went to the point his letter had spoken of, which overlooked the "diggins," and, clearing away the snow, began with pick and shovel to dig the grave. It was nearly dark when he had finished his sad labors, for he was weak, and his overstrained limbs were stiff and aching. Enfeebled as he was, he felt he must take another day for the burial, and he limped back to the cabin.

That night, as darkness fell, his loneliness came over him with such a sense of its awful meaning as he had not felt before. The silence, unbroken, save by the occasional snapping of the fire and his own movements, gave him that awesome sensation the presence of death inspires; but now that his mind had in a way recovered from the appalling fact, the future, a future there without Zeb, in utter loneliness, without companionship, seemed something he could not endure. He would, after the sad duty of the morrow was over, leave Yellow Pine Basin forever, and go somewhere, anywhere, in search of other human beings, but his promise to Zeb prevented. No, he must remain there to carry out the last wishes of his friend.

Then his mind went back to the old mountaineer, who, in his blankets, lay a cold, dread, awful reminder of his duty. What a nature was his! he thought. All of it many would think so common and so rough, but through the rudeness of it shone out to Bud the man, tender, considerate, loyal, fearless.

Every day he could remember emanated from it some touch of gentleness, some kindly, cheery saying, some hearty act of thoughtful care for him, and then came to him flashes of the stern, just, brave spirit that, under all the trials of a life so exacting in its calls on manhood, was always ready, eager, to respond in determined purpose, honest action, and brave deed.

As he sat he thought, "Why should the poor dead flesh there be repellent to me, when it was the frame of a spirit so gentle and so true, whose last words to me, written while his strength was fading, were so full of kindly feeling?" And getting into his bunk, he drew the blankets over him and slept.

In the bright sunshine of the morning, for the storm was over, he carried to the open grave the poor remnant of what had been so much to him. Weighted with the sad load he bore, Bud's lame, strained frame staggered on, but more weary and sore was the heart within. Tenderly he laid him in his final resting place, his shroud but a red woollen shirt, his coffin but the blankets from his bed.

Among his belongings Bud had a Book of Common Prayer, and over the senseless form he read the solemn service of the Church, dropping the earth as the words "dust to dust" were spoken. He filled in the earth, smoothed it down, covered the mound with heavy stones, and with a last look at the grave, Zeb was left to his sleep.

Green grow the grass over you, Zeb. Let the flowers bloom and fade, let winters come and go, and springs and summers wax and wane. The body will rot, and the elements of which it is composed go back to the earth from which they came. But you were something more than nitrogen and oxygen and calcium and phosphorus; you were kindness and loyalty, faith and courage. You have returned to earth all she ever gave you; paid the debt to nature, as they say, and have left behind you a legacy to all men—not gold, nor lands, nor bonds, nor stock, but that greater treasure, the memory of a true man. Your heirs are all who knew you, many who did not, for who can tell how far-reaching is example of gentle kindliness and manly bearing, the seed of which, planted in one heart, may bear fruit through unborn generations?

The type of man which you were will soon pass from us altogether. The history of our great West, such as you have made; and when the last of the pioneers shall have gone, we will be losers. In the heat and the cold, in privation and danger, through thirst and hunger and blood, have men like you won a great empire to civilization.

Poet and tale-teller have passed you by, and amid the glitter and the tinsel of the world have seen you not. Gold has no sheen nor shimmer but, turn it as you may, every ray of light that strikes it shows it always the same. Over that stone-covered mound in Yellow Pine Basin let one who knew you well, and others like you, stand a moment, and to the virtues of a class whose failings and shortcomings he well knew the why and wherefore of, as like a haze they pass in his mind over the fierce, hot sun of your brave purpose, of your valor, your determination, your manhood, your loyalty, your faithfulness, pay modest tribute such as grave of Cæsar or Napoleon could not call from him.

One can picture to himself the loneliness of that

night after Zeb's burial. Who of us has not felt what he felt, hardly less acutely because friends were near and gave us sympathy as they themselves suffered?

"I have been," Bud said to himself, "floating along; now I have before me a work to do," and he read again Zeb's words. "I will go do it. Zeb has taught me so much, I will do his wishes here. I will go back and face my trouble, and surely I must win. There must be justice that will not allow an innocent man to be thus branded."

As before his lonely fire he sat that night, came back to him the simple old man and the strange meeting with one who had been so unobtrusive yet so faithful a teacher. He could call up a hundred things Zeb had said which, now he knew, were meant to strengthen and to guide him.

"By the sweat of his brow shall man earn his bread." Labor has more to its account than the earning of bread, and so Bud found.

A fierce desire for work came over him, and early and late he labored. As spring came on and the snow under the warming sun gave out its water, he, as Zeb had taught him to do, utilized its power and swept through the boxes and the race great masses of gravel, catching gold in abundance, and adding to what had already been secured, sack after sack. At last he found that ahead of him the gravel no longer contained anything but minute light particles of gold, and going back he sluiced into the boxes the sides of the cut, prospecting it as he went, finding that the rich ground was only a narrow strip through which they had run the cut.

It was into June, however, before he had exhausted

all the rich gravel, but when he stopped work, twelve sacks of gold-dust were filled, and another half full, and taking Zeb's estimate as to weight, he thought he had in them about twelve or thirteen hundred ounces. He buried the sacks and concealed the deposit as best he could.

There were the horses to get up, and going down where they were, he caught them, Bally coming to the salt; and following Zeb's injunctions to the letter, he said, "Bally, Zeb is dead; he is gone." Was it imagination? He fancied the old horse changed; he would look at him with eyes following his movements, and allowed him to handle him as he pleased. He was fat, as were the others, but a change had come over him. He followed him like a dog, never kicking nor biting at him.

In a few days Bud had them all at the cabin, and he saw Bally go to the grave and smell and paw. Like a dog he lay by it all night, feeding near it from time to time.

The next day Bud placed a rough-hewn timber at the head of the grave, and wrote on one smoothed side, "Zeb, died March, 1882."

As he wrote "Zeb," he paused a second for the name, but he had never known it. It was a surprise to him he had never thought of another name; it astonished him; but so it was, only "Zeb," nothing more.

That day he made all ready, and early the next morning he took Zeb's poor belongings with his own. On one horse he placed the gold-dust, packed up, placing Zeb's saddle on Bally, and his own on his bay.

He went up to the grave, and on his knees before

it, tears in his eyes, bade a last good-by to the dead, mouldering form beneath the rocks and earth.

He looked his last on Yellow Pine Basin as one does on some place which he knows has been the theatre where unwonted experiences have acted out their changing phases, and back into the great world he started.

The streams were still high, and his progress was retarded by them, as also by the snow, which, in the higher country he passed over, was still covering the ground. Stanley Basin was a morass, and along the foothills he picked his way. Then came the swollen Salmon, with its strong current to be crossed.

On the bank he tightened his packs, and though it ran wild and turbulent, he put his horses in to swim it. The main Salmon, which there is wide and shallow at low water, in the early summer is a nasty stream to swim, except where certain stretches, known to the initiated, slow up the speed with which in most places the torrent makes its way.

Bud knew nothing of the river in its then condition; he knew it must be crossed, and though he was not one to falter when a thing was to be done, there was that in the swift rush of water that made him, as he stood only knee deep, look anxiously ahead for what seemed the best place of attack.

Zeb's things, his old gun among them, and a few of his own, were on a strong roan, and the gold with them; other things, his blankets and tools, were on the other two packs. He rode his bay, and old Bally bore only Zeb's empty saddle.

With some driving and urging all the animals were headed in what seemed the best course to cross. The water, knee deep, was soon belly deep on the horses, and then up on their sides, nearly to Bud's knees. Their feet left the bottom and all were swimming, the current getting stronger; soon it became more rapid, and as they neared the middle of the stream it was furious. Bud began to be dizzy and had to shut his eyes. The horses, heads up stream, could hardly breast it and hold their ground, but all fought bravely for the other shore.

The swirl of a strong eddy caught Bud's horse and turned him around. As he opened his eyes he could see the animals separated, and all in the power of the water that was slowly, in spite of their struggles, carrying them down stream. The little black, as he looked, rolled over and over in the water, and he saw him no more. Just then the water caught his own horse, and as it rolled him over, Bud freed himself, and was buffeting the mad rush, when he saw Bally at his side, and caught his mane, and then the pommel of the saddle. Horse and man struggled for life. Bally, stout swimmer though he was, could hardly hold his own; another stronger current caught them, tearing Bud from his hold. Down stream went man and horse, but some chance guidance of the water threw Bud against a tree top which the floods had carried down and lodged against the bank; he caught a limb, and at last dragged himself out of the water. Below him, when he could look about, he saw the bay had reached the shore, and beside him was the roan, but he could see nothing of the others.

Bud went down the stream to where the horses were, weak and trembling from the contest with the river and the icy coldness of the water, which benumbed him also.

He searched along the bank for the others until, in a small bay-like indentation of the shore, in the still water that there, out of the tossing, plunging current, had settled quietly, he saw old Bally.

In his struggles the saddle had parted from him, and the good old horse lay dead. "Gone to Zeb," Bud said, as he looked on the old companion of his friend.

He remembered how Bally had saved him in all probability from death. Ever since he had taken him from the winter range he had been a changed horse. All his capricious viciousness had left him, and as if he knew Bud was, in a way, Zeb's representative, he acted in so quiet a manner that Bud was astonished; and then his coming to him in the water, for it seemed as if there had been purpose in it, together with Zeb's love for him, and that in a way he felt himself the guardian of the old horse, all made him feel very tender. "You shall not miss a grave," he said; "well have you deserved it." He could find nothing of the black, but the gray he thought he saw as far away as he could see the river, floating in the middle, down the stream, and beyond his reach.

Going back to where old Bally lay, Bud camped, and started to dig a big hole to serve as a grave for the old horse. That day he could not finish it, but on the next he did, and the other horses dragged Bally into his grave. Bud filled it up and left him.

A few days' travel brought him where he could sell his gold-dust, and from it Bud obtained $22,758.33. He packed the few articles that Zeb had, and that had been saved from the waters, and directing the package to James Peasley, Poseytown, Indiana, put it in the express office. He purchased from Wells, Fargo a draft on New York, to his own order, for $11,379.17, sold his horses, and gathered together for a journey to New York his own things, articles that would in after times have to him interest and value, and with them Zeb's gun carefully boxed, taking at the same time drafts on New York for his own share of the gold-dust less what money he needed for his journey.

He wrote a long letter to James Peasley, telling him of Zeb's death, and enclosing the draft and Zeb's letter, mailed it, and that night the East-bound train bore away Zeb's partner.

CHAPTER XIII.

It was a hot summer day in a little Indiana village, without a breath of cooling air to neutralize the fervid rays of the scorching sun; the hour of noon had come; the steam whistle of the corn-sheller at one end of the town—it had been named "Poseytown"—sounded in blacksmith and carpenter shop, and in village store, and in such other shops and business places as there were, as well as in the modest, white-painted dwelling-houses, the dinner hour.

The little hum of life that from shops and corn-sheller had buzzed, sank away, and the steps of men as they went to the midday meal, and the creaking of a gate, or the sharp snap of one as it closed after the incomer, only varied the monotonous droning of bee and grasshopper, as with their tiny voices they emphasized the sleepiness of the sultry July noonday.

Inside many village homes the meal was on the table; the female community, warm from their culinary labors with meat and vegetables over hot cooking-stoves, were calling lingering man and boy together, to take their seats before the homely fare.

A little belated came limping down the main street the village justice of the peace, his big cane striking the unpaved sidewalk with unusual hurry, and ringing on the dry planks that here and there some householder had placed before his home—an elderly man, precise in his old-fashioned dress, with his blue swallow-tail coat, and its bright brass buttons flat and polished, covering a thin, angular frame; his nankeen trousers, starched to stiffness, concealing some imperfection in his legs, which his lame, halting gait indicated.

The big, black soft felt hat shaded with its wide brim a face clean shaven, that bore in its every line that consciousness of importance and authority, that half-official, half-fatherly interest and concern for everything and everybody which comes from a law-established power over the ill-doers of the community, and a more or less intimate knowledge of the business, financial standing, and secrets of almost every one. Such smattering of the laws of the State he had as, added to native good sense, made him a worthy incumbent of his office, in which, with strict justice and impartiality, he weighed the evidence and gave his judgments. An honesty and good nature that was as methodical and precise in its expression as the man himself, and a clear-headedness and shrewdness that all knew and respected, made him in a way father-confessor to the village and the country around, and friend and counsellor to the neighborhood.

Long holding of his office, for he had been justice for a quarter of a century, had made him somewhat arbitrary and opinionated; power and station have that influence. If you can fine your neighbor two dollars for allowing his pigs to run in the street, and he himself, should he on some occasion of hilarity overstep the bounds of strict decorum, and on his homeward way, with lusty song and loud-mouthed shouting, disturb the slumbers of the people, five dollars for such unseemly conduct, it does lift you above others; it is human nature; you can't help it; you feel the sense of power you have, and, feeling it, you show it.

But there are powers behind thrones, and such a power was behind Judge Peasley, and like a culprit going into his own court, he entered the gate and hobbled up the gravel walk to his door.

"What ails you, Jim Peasley? Corn fritters for dinner, and they all burnt to a crisp with your coming so late. You'll drive me to my grave with your aggravating ways. It's a wonder I'm alive to-day. Where have you been? What have you been doing that you didn't know 'twas dinner time? I wouldn't speak, but here it is, day after day. You've no consideration for me, and I slaving for you."

The Judge might have said that his being late was a most unusual event; but, wise from experience, he refrained from speech.

"There you are, standing like a fool. Can't you speak, I say? What have you been doing? But it's no use to ask you anything; some men tell their wives something, but you never do."

"Why, mother, I was reading some letters, and I got to thinking how something had best be done. I didn't know it was so late. I'm sorry, I am."

"Oh, yes, you're sorry; but that's all the good it is. What are you palavering about? Why don't you sit down and eat? You'd drive a woman to the asylum, and there I'll go, Peasley; little you'd care either, and me that's worked for you twenty year."

"Now, don't, mother, don't. Why don't you get that colored girl to help you?"

"Yes," sniffed Mrs. Peasley, "that's just like you,

wanting me to have more work and more worry. It's enough, goodness knows, to have you to worry me, without having an idle, chattering girl around to smash the dishes. I manage this house, and I'll thank you to let me alone."

The Judge ate in silence, as Mrs. Peasley did not do, for she was full of real and imaginary troubles, and when there were no real ones at hand, her imagination conjured up all possible ills that might come to her.

Born and bred in New England, as a school-teacher she had drifted into Indiana, and when somewhat mature, with the schoolmistress habit well fastened upon her, the Judge had wooed and won.

A natural tendency to scan the horizon for any speck of cloud, and an ability to create from it a tempest as soon as her eye fell on it; a thinly disguised contempt for the ideas and opinions of every one but herself, and a never-failing command of language, which she could use with most unpleasant effect, made the rough shell which concealed much kindness of heart and good sense. To her failings the Judge, if not blind, had thought it better to be deaf; her virtues he saw most clearly, and respecting her insight into human nature, a quality that he had found her to possess in an eminent degree, often took her advice in matters outside of ordinary affairs.

"I had two letters this morning, mother," he said, "and I don't know how to do what I must do, or how to do it in the most considerate way, I mean. I had an old friend, we were boys together. He left here and went to California thirty years ago or more. To-day I have heard of his death, and I have a letter he wrote me before he died, too. I liked him as a boy, and his course has been such that I have for him great respect; yes, I think I never respected a man more. You never knew him, for he left here before you came to Poseytown. His people, so far as I know, are all dead, but he has those here who were his care, though they never knew it; and how I'm to tell it all to the woman, I don't know, mother. It's such a sad story, and it will come on her so unexpectedly; she's forgotten the man, I dare say."

"Why, father," as she called the Judge when in her better moods, "the woman, you say? Tell me all about it."

"There's such a lot of money comes with it all, that I'm to give her, and I'm not to tell who the woman is. I don't know as I ought to tell as much as I'm going to.

"Suppose, mother, that before you met me some man should have loved you, and you had told him to go his way, and I had been a worthless drunken, shiftless man, and this man who had loved you had gone, and when he heard that your life was what such a man would make it, and you and your children were in need, should have gotten a friend to lie for him, and tell you that some old debt owed to your father was to be paid you, and this man should year after year send his friend money as he could, and have that money paid on this lying debt, paid to you, and for nearly sixteen years that money had kept the breath of life in you and your children—money that came from the hardest toil and through terrible dangers and privations—and in all this time he had never spoken to you, written to you, seen you, and dying had sent you a big lot of money. How would you have this told you?"

"Don't tell me any more, father, don't. Go to this woman and tell her just what you have told me, just as you have spoken it, and tell her that this dead man's secret—what a man he was!—is now only hers and yours, and that no man or woman knows of it— say that, father, that no woman knows of it—but you two, or ever will.

"I'm glad you told me of this, father. It is good to know such men have lived, but I would not hear more. It would be sacrilege. What a man he was!"

Then tears came to her, and she fell a-crying.

"Yes," said the Judge, with a husky voice, "he was a man."

In every community, no matter how small, there seems always to be some good-for-nothing man, whose weakness works injury only to himself and those who, unfortunately, are dependent on him, while the contempt he is looked upon by all is in a measure neutralized by a certain good humor and consideration for everybody outside of his own family circle. When young he was a general favorite, hail-fellow well met, too weak to have either enemies or strong friends; with few opinions of his own, readily falling into the general sentiment of those about him, he acquired the negative liking of all. No gathering of young folks was complete without him, and he was held up by fathers and mothers as a model to other boys whose activity of mind and positive natures made them combative of the ideas of their elders and less submissive than was he.

. Such a young man had been Ellery Simmons, a son

of well-to-do people, whose idol he was. Nature had endowed him with good looks and a pleasing address, which, added to prospects most promising and a seeming absence of vices, made Poseytown a unit in sentiment when he married Jane Richards, a village belle.

Life seemed to open to these young people a future of comfort, success, and happiness. Jane was a girl everybody liked; she was bright and good and pretty, and Poseytown settled down to the feeling that the match was a most appropriate one.

It was hardly a year before Jane found her husband was a drunkard. He wasted the patrimony left by his parents, who died a few months before the wedding. In wild speculation and riotous living his little fortune went. Poor girl, she did all she could to restrain him. He would promise amendment, only, perhaps, within the same hour to yield to a weakness that seemed to drag him down in spite of himself. A child had come to them, and neither mother nor child could change the downward course the poor weak fool had started on.

She saw him day after day sinking deeper and deeper into that slough out of which the strong man may struggle, but the weak one never. Her pride and her love made her keep such secret counsel with herself as to-day keeps many a fair, sweet young wife in village, town, and city. But there came a time when she felt the need of some help, some advice, to stem the current which she saw was wafting them all to poverty and want. The child she had, and another one soon to come, demanded of her that she do something, try something—what, she did not know; how, she did not know.

In the first year of her married life her mother died, and with her went the small annuity which, in the simple life they led, had been ample for the modest needs of mother and daughter; died thanking Providence for the assured comfort and well-being of her girl, that she felt had been guaranteed by the marriage. Jane's father had died years before, and she had but a hazy remembrance of him.

To whom should she so naturally turn in her troubles for fatherly advice as to Judge Peasley, her mother's old friend? And so one day she went, and into his kind heart poured the woes and fears of her life. With ready sympathy the Judge tried by friendly admonition to stop young Simmons, but with no good result; he promised everything, only to promise again and fall. At last want came on Jane, and, taking up her burden, she fought for her home and her children the same old fight that, since there were men and women, the weaker sex have waged when self-respect and little ones were to be maintained by their own exertions, hampered by some clog of husband and father.

The Judge, writing to an old friend about this time, mentioned as a matter of news this sad condition of one they both knew, and spoke of it all most feelingly. He had, as his circumstances allowed, and in ways Jane's pride could make no objection to, put in tangible form his sympathy; his wife, with the good sense and consideration she had, directing the channels of such helpful aid. Many an unnecessary article of needlework had she gotten Jane to make, and paid for it the money they had to give.

Some weeks after, the Judge received a letter, and

back to his office after his dinner he limped for this letter.

A methodical man he was, and in his old iron safe he had a bundle of letters which he took out, looking at the bottom one and some others; and then going back to the first one he read as follows:

"PRESCOT, ARIZONY, *May* 3, 1868.

"DEER JIM:

"I put in this letter 230 dollars. Wells, Fargo has offices everywhere; they'l pay ye the cash, no feer on 'em, ther all rite. Jim, ye can help me, and ye must do it. Ye mind when I was in Injianny after the war; ye mind I was there a long time, and why did ye think I was so long? I'll tell ye, Jim.

"Ye know how all the folks was glad to see me, and Miss Richards was that kind to let me bord in her house. Jane was the puttest woman I ever see, and tho I was so much older, somehow a seeing of her every day I fell in love with her; yes, Jim, I did; she was so good and kind to me I was Fool enuf to think she'd care for me. What a dang fool I was! Well, I hung round for months, and she was so kind and hearty and plessent that I got the big head, and one night I ask her to be my wife. She didn't know, how could she, that I was so gone a-lovin of her, and she laffed at me, and said it couldn't be; I was too old for her. Ther never was nothing hit me like that. I see what a cussed fool I was. Jest then somebody come in, and I walked out, I wanted air so bad. As I come down the step ther was a-layin on it a blue ribbin Jane had worn in her hair. I put it in my pocket and I've got it yet.

"I left kind o' sudden, ye will remember, Jim, and that's why.

"I never loved no woman but her; I never will; but, Jim, I do.

"'Twon't make no diference, and she's forgot me by this, and ye won't tell nothing. When I heered she was married and all so well with her, I was glad, tho it cut me, Jim, I won't deny that cut me. My heart is worryed over her, and 2 little ones, too. John Richards was a man nobody didn't know nothing 'bout much, and course he died, so she didn't know much 'bout him, and Miss Richards she's dead. Now, I want ye to lie for me, Jim; yes, Jim, I want ye to lie to Jane, and tell her that some man owed her father, and had wrote to you that he's going to pay his debt soon as he can; that he can't pay much at a time, but he'll keep a-chippin' in on it, and that on no count he wants it nowen who he is, as he oughter paid it before, and it's on his conscience like. Tell enny yarn ye like, that if so be ye think ye have a better lie than I give ye.

"Them 230 dollars ye give her right away, and I'll wressle up more pretty soon. I'm a goin to Mexico, and I'll raise something soon as I can, and send ye. If I'm kinder slow sometimes—luck goes agin a man a while, ye know, Jim, and then it goes with him—don't ye let her want, and I'll make it up to ye, Jim, sure's I live, Jim.

"I'll send ye more soon as I can. Don't make no talk 'bout that lie; its all rite. Ye don't know but 'twas so. I mite have owed old man Richards. I say I did; that's enuf for ye.

"Ye do this, Jim, and ye'll do more for me nor enny man can.

"Hopein as yer all well, no more from yer friend,
            "ZEB BEAN."

Fifteen years before, and with some qualms of conscience, for he was a plain, truthful man, the Judge had gone to Jane, and told her of this windfall from her dead father's debtor. Of course she wondered at it, and speculated much as to how great was this debt, and how certain might be its repayment, for it meant everything to her. The Judge told her that he had a pretty good idea it was a large debt, and he felt quite sure that unless the debtor should die he would continue his payments, and that was all he could or would say.

As time went by, and year after year enough came from the unknown debtor to keep her in comfort, she grew less anxious about it, and came more and more to depend on these moneys. Every six months or so the Judge would get a remittance, sometimes from Mexico, sometimes from Montana, and sometimes it would be so delayed that he would advance such amounts as were needed to keep Jane, her children, and worthless husband, and then would come money to repay him, and more. Once Zeb had sent him three thousand dollars. The Judge had put it on bond and mortgage for her where it would pay seven per cent.

With such love as she could give, Jane held to her husband, whose gentleness of temper made his failings less hard to bear than they otherwise would have been. She nursed him when sick, and she cared for him when well. He was never violent or abusive, but always a drag and a mortification to her, and grew gradually into that listless, indolent, lounging creature, the village loafer. She had tried to awaken in him pride, ambition, energy, but there was no germ to call into life; she had toiled and prayed for and with him, but loafer and lounger was he by nature, his only vice or passion a craving for liquor, and his only thought how by hook or crook he might obtain it. He had, it was true, an affection for his family, if one might dignify the feeling by calling it affection, but, as time went on, it had gotten to be an effect of a kind of natural good feeling and habit, rather than a living, actuating thing. He simply lived along, as does some worthless cur who has fallen into a home where all that is expected of him is to be of a decent temper, and, like one, he moved about in his aimless round of lounging, careless indolence.

What bitter trial and pain had come to wife and mother she kept to herself, and in the judicious care and education of her three children she took such pleasure as her life could give her. The respect of all she had, for every community recognizes the worth of the woman who leads such a life, and in it bears herself with womanly fortitude and courage. The repayment of the old debt, made as it was, had enabled Jane to bring up her children well, fitting them to enter life with some provision of education and rearing that might give them a vantage in life's struggle and make them independent when the remittances should stop; she had laid by a little from these moneys, and owned her small house, and with her three thousand dollars at interest she felt herself in such modest circumstances as made her somewhat easy.

CHAPTER XIV

For years, and at intervals of a few months' time, Judge Peasley had come and taken Jane's receipt for the sums of money sent to her. He was a month or two late, and she had mildly wondered at it. But now he was coming in the gate, and she went to open the door for him, ushering him into the neat little parlor, dark as a cell after the outer sunshine, until the blinds were opened.

"Jane," said the Judge, "I've come to tell you something, and when you hear it I want you to put yourself in my place. I think I did right, but it don't seem so quite, and I've never felt just easy about it for the part in it I've had.

"It's a strange story, Jane, but it's all brought and brings good to you. I have some letters I'm going to read to you, and they will tell this story.

"A good many years ago I had this letter sent to me, Jane; and because the writer was an old friend, and because it seemed the only way to do what he wished and I wished, I have acted a lie for over fifteen years. You see it was written in '68—yes, May 3d, '68. I'll read it, for the writing's poor, and I know it;" and taking out his spectacles and wiping them with his red bandanna, taking a longer time than was necessary in doing it, as if he was loath to open the matter, he at last adjusted them as Jane Simmons said:

"It must be about that old debt, Judge."

"Yes, Jane," he said, "it is about that old debt."

Slowly and carefully he read the letter from Zeb, and when he finished it and laid it on the table, Jane's face was white. As he read, it had all come back to her—Zeb's evident admiration; his awkward attentions; his speaking to her one evening and asking her to be his wife; her hasty, contemptuous refusal of him; she had regretted speaking so brusquely to him, and for a year or two it lay on her conscience, but she had forgotten him, had not thought of him for years. She saw it all, the love that thought not of itself, whose tender, far-away arms had reached out and shielded her and hers all those long years, and her tears came thick and fast.

Before she could speak, the Judge said, "Jane, I would not have read you this, but Zeb Bean is dead. He died in Idaho, and his last thought was of you."

"Oh, Judge, Judge!" she cried, "how could you do this, to make me all this time believe it was my father's money, my money, that came to me? Not but I am grateful to this man whom I treated so heartlessly; not that it isn't something a woman feels to have such devotion shown her, so kind, so persistent, so steadfast. Not that I don't see what a man he was, and from my heart I thank him and respect him; but I could never have taken it. I could never have taken the money."

"No, Jane, you wouldn't take it. Zeb knew that, and I knew it; but it was best you should. Let me talk to you, Jane, as I would to my child, my own child. You know, and I know, it was a matter of remark here in Poseytown that you in a way encouraged poor Zeb; that you led him on in the thoughtless way pretty girls, as you were then, you know, do. With most men it don't matter much, but Zeb was a man that was truth itself. He believed your little heartless, thoughtless, innocent lies, and he grew to think you might love him, and like a man he asked you to marry him. You laughed at him, and like a man he went away. Your folly and your cruel laugh and words did not change him; such a man does not change. You were in his heart, and in all the wild hard life he led he kept you there. You were his thought; he worked for you, went through such peril and privation as no one knows for you. Yes, Jane, you and your children, that you might live and be comfortable. Save you and me, no man, no woman, knows this story, and you only know it now.

"Do you tell me, Jane, that you would be so cruel as to regret that, though you did not know it, the thought that he was caring for you was his comfort? You are not that heartless."

"Oh, Judge, don't talk so to me!" and her face grew hard and stern. "You know, Judge, my life. God forgive me if I contrast this man and that. I am humiliated. It has all come on me so suddenly. I have been living all this time on the bounty of this man, and shame comes over me that it is so. But that I don't see what a noble heart this man had, that I don't appreciate what he has done, and wish to do what he would have—for you say he's dead, Judge—you must not believe. I, and for the children he has been father to when they had none, bless his memory. Do you know, Judge, how a woman must feel to have had such a lifetime of silent love thrown around her? What a man he must have been! And you say he is dead, Judge."

"Yes, Jane, he is dead. Let me read this letter next, before I come to the one telling how he died. This, Jane, is written from Yellow Pine Basin, Idaho, and there is no date on it; the other letter will tell under what circumstances it was written."

"Deer Jim:

"I'm here with my pardner, a young man than whom there ain't no better.

"We've struck diggins that's like to be dang good. I'm a'most sixty, tho I don't in no wise feel like I warnt as good as new; but I've been a-thinking that things is likely to come to enny man, and I've had Bud here, my pardner, promise if ennything chances to me, he'll send this yer letter and the money that comes from my half of the claim to ye. He'll do it. I'll bet my life on him. He's squar, and the likliest man I ever see, 'cept Yank.

"Ye know what to do with the money if it amounts to ennything, as I think it will. Do ye take out enuf to pay off that morgige ye have on yer farm ye bought of old man James. It's only the right thing, for all ye've done and the good friend ye've been to me, Jim.

"The rest of it, do ye take and put somewhere to hire where 'twill be safe for her. If I live, I'm going East next summer, and I'll see ye somewhere and fix it with ye. I won't see her, a course, but if ennything chances to me ye'l git the money, and when ye've taken out what I say, ye fix it all right for her. I'd kinder like her to know I had loved her and thought on her so long, but mebbe 'twouldn't be well. Tell her or not, when I'm dead; 'twon't matter one way or t'other.

"O God, I hope 'twill be considerabel dust we'll git. I'd die easy if I knew she was fixed.

"She's been on my mind all the time, Jim. I've had dang poor luck, and hain't did by her what I wanted, but mebbe I've helped 'long.

"Ye've been good friend to me, Jim, and ye'll do this case I die, which I don't in no way look for, only ther's a chance, ye know, and it's better have things settled.

"I'm peart and comfortable, taking real comfort with my pardner Bud. I'm well, as I hopes all is in Injianny.

"Zeb Bean."

The sobbing of the woman and his own thoughts made the Judge's eyes dim, as he reverently folded up the letter and laid it with the others.

"This letter came," he said, "enclosed in one I received from Frank—Buddington," as he turned the page to make sure of the name. "This man was Zeb's partner he speaks of, and it enclosed also a big sum of money for me to give you;" and he read:

"Pocatello, Idaho, *June* 25, 1883.
"James Peasley, Esq.,
    "Poseytown, Indiana.
"*My dear sir:*
"It is my sad duty to inform you of the death of one greatly endeared to me, and with whom I spent several months in close companionship—months that during my life will be marked in my memory as filled with all that the best of companions, the truest of men could do to make them sweet in the remembrance and fruitful in good to me.

"Intimate as were our relations, I knew him by no other name than Zeb, and can speak of him only as I do.

"Some time previous to his death he requested me,

in case of accident to him, to write you and to send you, as I do in this letter, whatever moneys might be his.

"In compliance with his request I enclose Wells, Fargo's draft on New York, endorsed by me, to you, for $11,379.17, such being what was his due.

"The circumstances of his death are as follows:

"Late last season Zeb and myself struck in Yellow Pine Basin, which lies on the middle fork of the Salmon, in the Territory of Idaho (I do not know the county), such indications of gold as induced us to spend the winter there in order to open up for profitable working, should it warrant, the claim which we had located.

"During the winter we began getting gold from the claim. Early in February Zeb was injured by the caving down of the bank of gravel in which we were working.

"He never recovered from the effects of this, having received some internal injury. He gradually grew worse, though his cheerful nature and his desire to make as light of his hurt as possible before me, prevented my at first realizing how serious was his case. When, however, I did begin to feel his danger, I made my way to the nearest doctor, who, owing to the difficulty and, perhaps for him, impossibility of taking so long and exhausting a trip at that season, declined to visit him; and with such remedies as he gave me, though with them he gave me little hope, I returned and found Zeb dead.

"I buried him where he had indicated in a letter he had left for me, and, so far as the circumstances and my lonely condition allowed, I decently and sorrowfully laid him to rest, marking his grave.

"I have also shipped you by express the few personal articles he died possessed of. To those who ever knew him and loved him they will be of value.

"My acquaintance with him was that of a few

months only, but in that time he grew into my affections, and I mourn him as a son his father.

"I feel that I have, and shall always keep with me, a memory of a man so true and tender and loyal that all my life it will be to me a lesson, an example.

"It would be to me a pleasure (if you should think it not incompatible with his wishes, for with me he was very reticent about his life) to have you write me of his history such facts as would tell me more of the man I knew so short a time, but whom I so dearly loved.

"I omitted saying that, according to his direction, I buried with him a little buckskin sack containing something, doubtless, which he greatly prized.

"He had in his hand, pressed to his heart, when I found him, a strip of faded blue ribbon, and under the hand and the ribbon a Grand Army badge. What he had pinned on his breast, and what his dead hand held, I did not disturb, and they were buried with him.

"I cannot give the exact date of Zeb's death, as I found him dead on my return. I can say, however, that it was probably about the 5th or 6th of March last.

"No opportunity has before this offered to give you this melancholy news, as the wild and uninhabited country prevented my having any means of communicating with you, and my promise to Zeb required me to work out what gold there was, on which, and it reaching you safely, his mind was firmly set.

"He displayed a feverish anxiety on this account, and the disposition you were to make of it seemed something that robbed death of any terrors it might have had for him.

"I am following out his directions to the letter, and do not doubt but you have such knowledge of Zeb's wishes and such desire to fulfil them as will, accompanied by this note I enclose, which he wrote some time before his death and asked me to forward, enable you to do all as he would wish it done.

"Stranger though I am, I wish to join with those friends who may mourn him. He was my friend, and in losing him I feel I have parted with a true man. His memory will be green in my heart always.

"Will you kindly acknowledge the receipt of this letter, its enclosures, and the package sent you by express?

"My address will be for some time, Metropolitan Hotel, New York City.

"Yours very truly,
"FRANK BUDDINGTON."

"He died alone," she said, between her sobs, "alone, and the ribbon, my poor old ribbon, in his hand."

"Jane," said the Judge, "you know it all now; we will talk of this money and how to invest it later. No one shall ever know of this, but I thought I must tell you."

"Judge," she said, "I thank you that you did; that woman is glorified to whom comes such a story. Leave me now, Judge; leave me now; we will talk again."

Putting in her hands the package of letters, only three of which he had read to her, the Judge went slowly out and limped towards home.

Jane Simmons threw her arms upon the table, and her tears came fast and hot.

In her life, so meagre in all that means so much to a woman, there had been something, after all, though she did not know it, something of manly devotion, something of love as strong as death, those letters told her.

At random she drew from the package, tied with its formal red tape, letter after letter, and through her tears read them. This from Montana, and enclosing three hundred dollars, with, "Ye know what this money's for, Jim. I hope she is comfortable and the little ones a-growing fine." This from Mexico, with an apology for sending only sixty-five dollars, and, "Luck's been agin me, Jim, but ye see she don't want, and I'll fix it with ye." This from Colorado, with four hundred and twenty-five dollars, and, "Take out what ye give her, Jim, and give her the rest. Write me a word, can't ye, how she is a-looking and a-feeling, and 'bout her children, Jim; I hankers to hear." This from Nevada, with its account of a "Wells, Fargo" check enclosed, and, "A manny thanks for what ye told me of her, Jim; ye don't know how it pleases me to here she's so peart." And so, through fifteen years they ran, dirty, some of them, and crumpled, written in language uncouth to her and in scrawling fashion, but all the same in spirit, all constant in their purpose. As she read them she could see the struggle for her this simple, faithful, loving heart had made.

Down on her knees she fell, and to One she worshipped poured out her heart in prayer. She rose and put the letters together, tying them with the tape again, and taking them with her went out of the room, carrying the secret of one man's constancy that would be to her all the rest of her life the most treasured possession of her heart.

One by one she read the old letters as she found herself alone to do it. Every one told the singleness of purpose, the absorbing interest in her, the tender, faithful love and care for her that through long years had actuated the man. She pictured his life, his lonely death. Constant to the end he was, his heart holding her to the last as did his fingers the old blue ribbon.

It was a bitter time for Jane, the few days that passed before the Judge called again. Not that she had ever loved this man; that, perhaps, made her reveries more painful; that so true and tender and constant a love should not have come to its reward seemed so sad, so cruel.

In indignation and soreness of heart, the man she had loved and this one came always before her. The weak, selfish drone, whose only ambition was by deceit, or often by cunning theft of her small moneys, to make himself a beast; and the strong, manly, tender, constant one, who all these years had been bread-winner for her and hers.

There was degradation in the thought of the one, but what of the other? Over her came again and again, as she thought of him, that scene of his lonely death in the wild country. Her imagination saw him grasping the ribbon and going out of the unloved life he had lived, as loyal to her as the soldier to his colors, that through storm of battle he carries while life lasts. But after days and nights of self-communion there fell on her something of the spirit of the dead man. "He bore his burden," she thought, "and bore it cheerfully; so let me bear mine." And the round of her daily duties she moved in, sadder in a way, happier in a way.

Once more the old Judge hobbled up and into her little home. She was calm now, and the Judge precise, methodical, business-like. "Here is the money," as he took from his pocket a draft, "$11,379.17," he said. "I would advise you, Jane, to put this money out at mortgage. I have found that John Stebbins must have some money; his big farm is good security for what you have. He has spoken to me, and I have said that I knew where the money is. I have found that he will for $11,375, give you a mortgage at six per cent. and running ten years for $12,000 on his property; this at six per cent. will give you seven hundred and twenty dollars a year, and with the interest from the three thousand dollars you have already at mortgage, which is at seven per cent., and returns two hundred and more dollars a year, will give you an income of nine hundred and thirty dollars a year, which, with your house, Jane, will make you comfortable all your life. Indeed, Jane, I have made out the papers, and John Stebbins will sign them as soon as you consent. I know of no better security you could have."

"But, Judge, out of this money something was to go to you."

"Yes, Jane. Zeb knew I had given a mortgage on my little farm, but that I paid off years ago, and I have nothing to take from it; and if the mortgage was still unsatisfied I wouldn't take it. There is a package sent me by express, also; only some old things Zeb had about him when he died, and they should go to you. Shall I send it here?"

"Yes," said Jane. "Anything that belonged to him should come here. Where else should they go?"

"Jane," said the Judge, "I will attend to this business, and when that is all done we will speak no more of it. The secret that Zeb so closely kept we will keep now. He would have had it so."

"Yes," said Jane, "I think he would."

That same day the package came to her. With tender hands she touched the mean things that showed so clearly the rough life Zeb had used them in—the patches on the old coat, the soil he delved in for her still here and there upon it; the hunting-knife so sharp and keen; the old Colt's revolver, and its leathern sheath and cartridge-belt, that told of long and constant use; his pipe, the mouthpiece gone, and the marks on the wooden stem where his teeth had held it; the Testament, and in it, "To my boy Zeb, from his loving mother," and some old letters from Judge Peasley; one in which he had written Zeb about her and her children, much worn, as if it had been often read. These, and a buckskin sack in which big needles and coarse thread, old buttons, and one silver dollar, one half dollar, with old cartridge-shells and little odds and ends of things, were all. But over them she cried, as in their eloquence they told her more of the details of Zeb's life.

She packed them all up again, and put them in the drawer where were the articles of dress her mother had last worn and a lock of gray hair from her dead head, the baby curls from her children, their first shoes, and such other precious things as she had. She locked the drawer and put the key in her bosom.

CHAPTER XV

Soon after reaching New York, Frank received this letter from Judge Peasley:

"Poseytown, Indiana, *July* 21, 1883.
"Frank Buddington, Esq.,
"Metropolitan Hotel.
"*My dear sir:*

"I acknowledge the receipt of yours of the 25th of the last month, with enclosures as follows: Draft on New York for $11,379.17 to my order; also a letter from my poor old friend Zeb Bean; also a package by express.

"The sad news has been softened somewhat by feeling that one so devoted to him as you evidently were, and so much loved by him as Zeb's letter to me tells me you were, did for him all that could be done.

"We were boys together, and aside from my liking for the man there were circumstances, for fifteen years only known to me, and now only to one other, which have made me honor the man and revere his memory.

"You will excuse me if I do not say more of what these circumstances were. It is Zeb's secret, and I do not feel justified in telling the story; suffice it to say that did you know it, you would feel, as I do, that Zeb was a man the like of whom are few, and you would appreciate a character than whom in all my life I have seen none more entitled to every good man's respect.

"Zeb Bean was born here, his parents coming from

North Carolina. In 1849 he went to California, and from his leaving here until immediately after the war I did not see him.

"In 1865 he came back here and remained several months. He had served during the war in an Iowa regiment, I think, and having been several times severely wounded recruited himself here.

"Since that time I never saw him, but heard from him from time to time. So far as I know, none of his family are living, and of course but few of his old friends.

"I am requested by one who greatly mourns him, and whom he held very dear, to say to you these words:

"'May God reward you for the tender care you gave to one whom I have so great reason to admire and reverence. Your name I shall always associate with what has been a joy as well as a grief to me. For your devotion to his interests I, who am benefited, regret that in this poor way only is it possible for me to faintly show a gratitude that I shall feel to my dying day.'

"We will leave this as it is. I feel it would have been Zeb's wish to have it so.

"Should you ever be able to come to our quiet town, it would give me great pleasure to see you and to express, what I cannot well do by letter, my appreciation of your courage and devotion and honesty.

"I think we are all better for having known Zeb. May life bring all my old friend would have wished you.

"Your obdt. servant,
"JAMES PEASLEY."

The clouds melted away and bright sunshine came to Frank. Vigorously and manfully he betook himself to his old occupations, strengthened, I think, by the experiences of his absence.

With years came to him the good things of life, the woman he loved, success. With loyalty and faithfulness he bears his part as husband, father, citizen.

I venture to say that in this year of our Lord 1896 there is no happier home in all the land than that of Frank Buddington. To his wife and him have come children, a good half dozen of them, bright, manly little fellows, and healthy, laughing girls. His broad shoulders but lightly feel the burden of great cares and responsibilities, and motherhood has only given to his wife increasing comeliness and beauty.

When the winter nights are long, young Frank says, "Tell us about Yank and Zeb, father," and his younger brother climbs on Frank's knee and all the prattle of the others stops. To the snows of Idaho and the old life there the father goes, and he tells over the story that all know so well, striving, as he tells it, to give some new aspect to the happy and interesting phases of it, and softening those that were hazardous and bitter, and might be harrowing in the recital. His mind goes back to the walk in the snow, to the finding of Zeb's cold body, to the lonely grave, and the influence on his life that came from all, and he says, as he closes, "Dear old Zeb, he would like to look at us to-night." And the mother says, "I wish he was here." And little Frank looks proudly up over the fireplace, where the old rifle hangs, and asks his father "if he thinks there will ever be another war."

"I wonder why he kept the blue ribbon," breaks in the mother's namesake.

"Eddication's good for boys, but the idee of the flag, that's the main p'int," says the father. "How true that is! You boys will have, in your time, I fear, to meet such changes as we can now only dimly see the coming shadows of. I hope the love of country and your country's flag that old Zeb hoped you would have, will be yours always. You can have no better education, and there are so many religions nowadays, that I'm not sure but that love of country and devotion to the Stars and Stripes is better than half of them.''

Every year, when the snows have melted and the waters have receded and the grass is green, come from Arizona and Colorado and Montana wandering prospectors, and they dig and pan and speculate as to where in Yellow Pine Basin is the old run of gold that Zeb and Bud had found, for the story of its getting has been noised about, and grows bigger with distance and with time. Every year they go away disappointed, and a new lot come again the next year, and so it goes, and I suppose will go. But if more gold is there than the stout roan bore through the sweeping current of Salmon River, Yellow Pine Basin holds its secret, holds it fast.

www.ingramcontent.com/pod-product-compliance
Lightning Source LLC
Chambersburg PA
CBHW031832230426
43669CB00009B/1320